I AM ALREADY SuccessfuL

Getting Motivated, Being Me

by Dennis Hooker

from

jist the job search people

Publisher: J. Michael Farr
Project Director/Interior Design: Spring Dawn Reader
Editor: Ann Holcomb
Editorial Assistant: Sara Hall
Production Editor: Lisa Farr
Cover Design/Spot Illustrations: Mike Kreffel

I Am (Already) Successful — *Getting Motivated, Being Me* • *Instructor's Guide*
©1991, **JIST Works, Inc.**, Indianapolis, IN

This book has a companion Instructor's Guide available separately from the publisher.

Send all inquiries to:
JIST Works, Inc.
720 North Park Avenue • Indianapolis, IN 46202-3431
Phone: (317) 264-3720 • Fax: (317) 264-3709

ISBN: 0-942784-41-3

Table of Contents

SECTION III—Your Success In The World   103

INTRODUCTION

Imagine that your friend has just told you, "Someday, I am going to be successful!" This puzzles you because you felt that your friend was already successful. Your friend is doing well, has a good attitude and enjoys a sense of personal accomplishment. Is it possible that your friend cannot accept that he or she is already successful?

The world around us seems to tell us that success is something we achieve, a triumph, or a victory. We are led to believe that "success" is an accomplishment of conquerors and champions. These conquerors are "victors!" That type of success creates those who were mastered, lost, or vanquished. The victorious leave behind victims.

But, "success" can have a more satisfying meaning. "Success" can mean enjoying your present status—which means liking and accepting your present state of mind. It is saying to yourself, "I am already successful. I do not have to do anything different. I do not have to wait for some accomplishment in the future to feel successful."

You will experience this more realistic attitude in *I Am (Already) Successful* by learning that you are already successful. Of course, there is room in your life and thinking for improvement, but success is already yours! This is not a positive-thinking pep talk, but is a fact!

In *I Am (Already) Successful*, you will discover what you like, how you feel, how you see others, and how they see you. These explorations will be pleasing and enlightening. You will feel successful every step of the way.

As you answer the questions on the pages of *I Am (Already) Successful*, you begin to see this as more than a simple book of worksheets. The responses you make map a journey through your very own experiences. *I Am (Already) Successful* provides the high octane fuel to power you on your trip. And as the author, I am your guide. I can show you some points of interest, but it is up to you to enjoy the trip.

Before we begin, however, I have some clear-cut ideas about the journey I want you to experience. So that you know where we are going, I share these "destinations" with you right up front.

1. You will discover that you are ALREADY successful! You do not have to become something or be somebody else to be a success.

2. The way you appear to others is usually how you THINK you are. In *I Am (Already) Successful*, you will learn how to let others see that you are successful.

3. You will discover that you can prosper without "being better" than someone else. Cooperation is better than competition. (If you feel competitive, try SELF-improvement—doing something better than YOU used to.)

4. You will acquire AN ATTITUDE of being already successful. You will probably "catch it" before you actually realize it.

5. When you feel successful, you can help those around you. You will find enjoyment, satisfaction, and personal growth in using what you have right now to help others. What you do in the future will demonstrate your interest in other people.

6. You will discover a new way to be with your teacher or leader. That person can now do more than just present material or give tests.

After you finish *I Am (Already) Successful*, you can express your opinion without worrying whether it is accepted or not. Your opinion is yours! You can use the words you already know and learn more words that "work" for you. You, working alone and as a member of small groups, will complete several projects. What you gain from these projects will be more rewarding than mere grades and applause.

I like to call these small groups "Think Tank" groups. The term "think tank" describes a place where people come to put their heads together and solve problems or discuss issues.

The projects in this book are tasks that you first work on alone and then share with others in your small groups. The results of many of these projects are then reported to the whole class. An example of this appears in the first simulation, when you decide whom to hire for your game-making corporation. After you come up with your own ideas, you coordinate your decision with others in your small group. Later, your group will help you explain or justify your decision to the total group.

My experience tells me that, as you make this journey, something even better is going to happen. I know that you will experience more than what I can imagine for you. Your own special thoughts and insights will occur when successful people (like you and the other members of your group) voyage together toward a similar destination. Have a good trip. I'll be right there with you.

What Makes This Book Unique

I Am (Already) Successful is BY you—and ABOUT you. This book is unique because it has no "right" or "wrong" answers. Nothing that you answer can be marked off! YOU decide how much energy you will invest in these experiences. Other members of your group will assist you by sharing their experiences with you and letting you share your experiences with them. If you think about the journey you take, you will find yourself getting better at expressing your ideas. Just remember, there are no "good" or "bad" answers, just how well you can express yourself.

A Conversation With The Author

The author (that's me, of course) of this book is also unique. I have never seen or experienced anyone just like me. But, I discover my similarity to you daily. Our alikeness is my incentive to share my ideas and feelings with you.

We are successful because we are working together on *I Am (Already) Successful* tasks. You may think that success comes only AFTER you complete tasks that are evaluated highly by yourself or someone else. Remember your working definition of "success" is to enjoy making the journey, not waiting until after you arrive at your destination. You are successful when you accept your success. Success does not depend on the quality of the project or the evaluation of others. When you accept your success, you can say, "I am already successful just because I am a worthwhile person and accept my own worth!"

I (the author of this book) am placing a dot at the end of this paragraph. Look for it. Remember, I placed the dot deliberately, on purpose and planned. It didn't just appear there. I sat down and said, "I'm going to put a dot there for the readers of *I Am (Already) Successful* to see." And I dotted it, printers printed it, and that dot was purchased for you. This dot is my thought to you. I am just on the other side of the dot. That is how close I am to you.

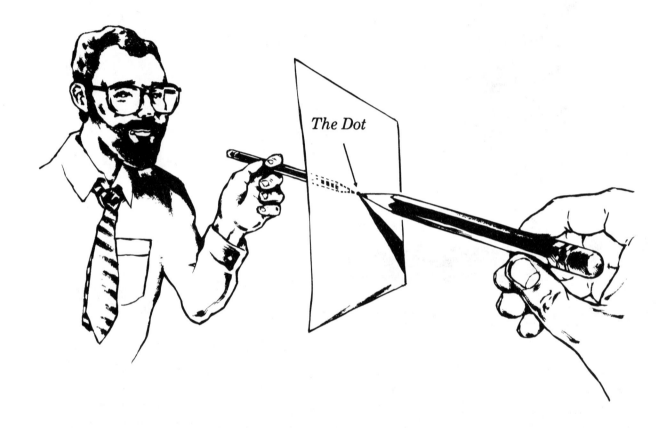

The Dot

✎ Put the point of your pen on the dot. Try to picture me. (I visualize you as I write each word.) Now tell me: How does it feel to be this close to the author?

_____

_____

_____

_____

_____

_____

_____

_____

✎ To help me know you better, tell me what you like to pick up and read:

_____

_____

✎ What kind of reading do you dislike?

_____

_____

✎ Your thoughts and ideas become "immortal" as you write them in this book. Someone a long time from now may read what you write. How does that feel? Does this change how you will write and what you answer?

_____

_____

_____

_____

_____

✎ What would you like to tell me? (You can even write me, if you like, at JIST Works, Inc., in Indianapolis.)

_____

_____

_____

_____

_____

How To Use This Book

This book is intended to be a dialogue between you and me. You may express yourself freely. There are no right or wrong responses to opinions and statements of feelings—only the appropriate time and place to express them. You will be doing this often in *I Am (Already) Successful*.

Thank you for your honest expression!

How This Book Is Organized

Each experience in *I Am (Already) Successful* is arranged according to the following divisions. Each division requires special energy on your part.

Challenge—You read and think about a problem or statement(s).

Explore—You work on tasks alone or in a small "think tank" group. This takes 15-30 minutes.

Putting It Together—You pull together loose ends and reflect on what you just finished. This gives you a unique energy to get ready for "spinning off." The time you spend depends on you or your teacher or group leader.

Spin Off—Your lines of thought branch out to other ideas or thoughts. The length of time spent spinning off depends on you or your leader/facilitator. Some of your individual and small group experiences are shared with the total group.

Being Successful Through Simulations

A simulation is an activity that gives you the feel and practice for doing the REAL thing. A video game, for example, can give you some of the experiences of driving a race car or flying an airplane. Astronauts simulate space flight by duplicating conditions that might be encountered in space travel. The difficulties in floating in near-zero gravity in space can be duplicated underwater by special apparatus attached to astronauts in waterproof suits. The astronauts learn to move as if they were actually in outer space rather than, in reality, underwater.

In a similar way, you will be asked to do simulations of the "Real World." A simulation is not artificial work. It is real! Thus, your tasks are real and demand the focused use of your energy!

All experiences in *I Am (Already) Successful* lead to one of three major simulations. The three simulations in this book are named:

I. THE GAME

II. THE BUSINESS

III. THE COMMUNIQUE

Each simulation absorbs several concentrated hours and demands what you already know about the world and yourself. Each simulation will challenge you to work cooperatively with other members of the Simulation Team. A simulation is the joint efforts of individuals working together and facing challenges as a team.

There are no pass or failures in a simulation. It is NOT a test. But, like most tasks, your progress is EVALUATED. You will judge what you have learned and how you applied yourself (sometimes called how you "grew as a person"). For example, if the Game in the simulation is a "commercial disaster," you may have discovered what the market does NOT want in a new game. You have successfully learned from an apparent "failure."

Moving On To Success

You are now ready to explore the first of three parts of this book. Over the remainder of this book, you will be asked to give your opinions about many issues. Please remember, there are no right or wrong answers—only differences of opinion.

In the next section, "You Are Unique," you will see why you are ALREADY very special—you are ALREADY a success!

SECTION I
You Are Unique

No one else is exactly like you—you are unique. You could be one of identical twins and still be unlike the other twin. Part of what makes you unique is the way you express yourself. The way you think and communicate is yours alone. Only you have the tones of voice, the mannerisms, the key phrases, and the patterns of thought that are you.

Your language is your vehicle for letting others know who you are, what you like and dislike, your plans for the future, and so on. You have already been successful in using the verbal and non-verbal symbols that make up language. How do I know? Because you are here and you are reading this book—something is working for you! In this first section, you will discover more about what you think and feel. You can increase your successes by communicating your ideas more effectively and by better understanding what others are communicating to you.

In Section I, you work toward the first simulation, the GAME. As you complete the activities in this section, you will identify opinions you already have and use your language skills to express those opinions to others. You will look at the word "success" and decide what it means to you.

Working within your small groups, you will decide the importance of things around you. What is important enough to you to make you angry? What could make you change your opinions? You will begin to see that you are important. You will see how you can use your success to help those around you.

At the end of this section is the first challenging simulation, the GAME. In it, you will combine what you know now with what you discover in this section. After the simulation, you will decide what you liked and didn't like about your performance in that simulation. Then you will evaluate how you performed.

OPINIONS

> **Challenge.** *"Don't bother me with the facts. My mind is already made up."*
>
> *Your opinion is what you think is true. An opinion may or may not be based on fact. An opinion is what you feel to be right or good.*

Explore.

✎ Decide if you agree or disagree with the following opinions. Circle "yes" if you agree and "no" if you disagree. Rewrite each "no" response to make it true for you. For "yes" responses give an example.

CHOICE	OPINION
Yes No	There will be some classes I won't like next year. _____
Yes No	I will always like my classmates. _____
Yes No	The world will probably get worse before it gets better. _____
Yes No	Some people are much better than others. _____
Yes No	I can usually tell before I talk to new persons if I will like them. _____
Yes No	People from some countries are easier to trust than people from other countries. _____
Yes No	I can spot a phony person a mile away. _____
Yes No	I seldom prejudge a person. _____

CHOICE	OPINION
Yes No	I'm sure I'll never make the same mistakes my parents made.
Yes No	It won't take much to make the world a better place.

Putting It Together. What do I really feel strongly about? What doesn't interest me? Am I used to giving my opinions? Why? Why not? Will I be graded for an opinion? How can presenting any opinion better let others know I am already successful? Do I really think I am (already) successful? Is this a hype job by the author? How is he right? How is he wrong?

Spin Off. Discuss each opinion with members of your class. Attempt to get others to see your point of view.

✎ Which opinion was the hardest to convince others of?

_____

_____

✎ Which opinion was the easiest to convince others of?

_____

_____

✎ Were you successful in changing anyone's mind?

_____

_____

TIME CAPSULE

> **Challenge.** *NASA wants you to place important information about yourself in a time capsule to be opened in 100 years. You decide to record your information on your computer, so you place a blank disk in the slot. You flip the switch to "On" and press the Enter key.*

Explore.

✎ "Type" information about yourself on the monitor below. When you are finished, read your screen to see if it says what you want to say.

I LIKE TO...

Challenge. *It is important (for both me and you) to know clearly what you like and dislike.*

Explore.

✎ In the activity that follows, thoughts, feelings, and actions are listed. For each one, mark in one column whether you RL (really like), L (like), D (dislike), or RD (really dislike) each one.

Likes and Dislikes Check List

____ show my feelings	____ be in new places	____ enjoy what is
____ patch up quarrels	____ adapt to change	happening "now"
____ be easy to know	____ make tough decisions	____ question decisions
		____ enjoy modern art
____ be complimented	____ feel loved	
____ speak	____ sympathize	____ prove myself
____ work hard	____ be a friend	____ follow a schedule
		____ read books
____ have choices	____ seek help	
____ be alone	____ make a statement	____ be criticized
____ visit museums	____ compliment	____ be bored
	someone	____ be anxious
____ point out mistakes		
____ be fair	____ be modest	____ be in a rut
____ be orderly	____ be deliberate	____ help myself
	____ be excited	____ criticize
____ have new friends		
____ decide own life	____ express myself	____ be able to see ahead
____ act casual	____ be logical	____ be imaginative
	____ have surprises	____ plunge into tasks
____ be superstitious		
____ argue	____ party	____ meet new people
____ be gentle	____ have emergencies	____ tolerate others
	____ create	____ be a follower
____ help others		
____ be cooperative	____ cause trouble	____ be expressive
____ feel loving	____ act impulsively	____ bring happiness
	____ make mistakes	____ be embarrassed

Likes and Dislikes Check List (continued)

____ think

____ discuss

____ study

____ plan my future

____ fix broken objects

____ notice strangers

____ make plans

____ get annoyed

____ be careful

____ be a boss

____ be scared

____ be confident

____ enjoy the unexpected

____ respect rights

____ like sunny days

____ be merciful

____ write

____ feel attractive

____ be open to suggestions

____ act detached

____ see rainy days

____ enjoy thrill rides

____ keep secrets

____ be spontaneous

____ worry

____ be in crowds

____ read quickly

____ go to movies

____ have common sense

____ be literate

____ be helped

____ be intimate

____ be spiritual

____ show leadership

____ travel

____ have hobbies

____ be surprised

____ act confident

Putting It Together. *I will review the check list and ask myself the following questions.*

✎ Do these form any obvious patterns about my likes and dislikes? If so, what are they?

_____

_____

✎ What surprises me?

_____

_____

✎ What is not a surprise at all?

_____

_____

Spin Off. *Share these patterns of likes and dislikes with your small group.*

THE PERFECT PERSON

Challenge. All people have an ideal, or perfect person. What characteristics make up the perfect person?

Explore.

✎ What does this perfect person looks like?

_____

_____

✎ How does the person act with loved ones?

_____

_____

✎ How does this person act around friends and classmates?

_____

_____

✎ What does the perfect person believe?

_____

_____

✎ Discuss the advantage and disadvantage of having a perfect person as an ideal.

_____

_____

Putting It Together. My personal comparisons to the perfect person.

✎ Specific ways I am similar to the perfect person.

_____

_____

✎ Ways I differ from this perfect person.

_____

_____

Putting It Together. *Discuss your ideal person's qualities with others in your group.*

✎ How do their ideas of "perfect" qualities differ from yours?

_____

_____

✎ How are they the same?

_____

_____

✎ Discuss the meaning of the saying, "When we put someone else on a pedestal, we have in some way diminished ourself."

_____

_____

_____

_____

Spin Off. *Work with your small group to design your perfect person. Be very specific! It can be a list or a narrative — such as "A Day in the Life of Our Perfect Person." You will share your group's Perfect Person with the total group.*

LANGUAGE

> **Challenge.** *"Language: the expression or communication of thoughts and feelings by means of vocal sounds...or written symbols for them to which meaning is attributed..." Webster.*
>
> *Imagine how human beings began using their voices for language.*

Explore.

✎ Write a scene describing how vocal language may have started. (Use extra paper if needed.)

_____

_____

_____

_____

_____

_____

_____

_____

_____

_____

✎ Now, create a scene that demonstrates how written language may have developed from spoken language.

_____

_____

_____

_____

_____

_____

_____

_____

_____

_____

✎ Define the following terms and show how each is uniquely different.

Expressive _____

_____

Fluent _____

_____

Literate _____

_____

Communicative _____

_____

Conversant _____

_____

> ***Putting It Together.*** *I will think of myself as a "language-enriched person."*

✎ How has my ability to choose the right words helped my social life? Job choices, home life, etc.?

Social life_____

_____

Job choices _____

_____

Home life_____

_____

Other _____

_____

> ***Spin Off.*** *Work with your group to think of ways to learn new words that can help your daily life.*

AS I SEE IT

> **Challenge.** *You have a chance to guess what is inside a box. You can use only the eraser end of a pencil through some holes in the box to feel what is inside. The box is covered with a cloth so no peeking can occur.*

Explore.

✎ Each Think Tank group is to punch six to eight holes in the sides of a small box (such as a shoe box). Each member will secretly place an object in the box that the others must guess. Each member gets one minute to poke and prod. State what you observe (For example: "It is soft and roundish."). Watch carefully everyone who tries, but do not talk. (You may not move or shake the box.) When each has taken a turn, the group must pool all observations and then make educated guesses to come to ONE conclusion—a consensus.

✎ Write the most important observations here.

OBJECT	OBJECT	OBJECT
_____	_____	_____
_____	_____	_____
_____	_____	_____

OBJECT	OBJECT	OBJECT
_____	_____	_____
_____	_____	_____
_____	_____	_____

> **Spin Off.** *Exchange your still-concealed objects with other groups. Watch them observe and come to a consensus. What process did the teams use to come to an agreement (if they did)? Who held out? Why? How?*

DAYDREAMING

Challenge. *Daydreaming is the creative flight necessary for planning future products or goals. Sometimes classroom daydreamers are frowned upon. You are told you cannot leave the classroom—even in your mind. You must sit with an intelligent look on your face even if you are "spaced out." A friend of mine once painted open eyeballs on his closed eyelids to look "aware."*

Go with me on creative flights of daydreaming fantasy. You can go anywhere, see, hear, and experience anything you want. There are no limits!

Explore.

✎ Read each phrase and write ANYTHING that comes into your mind.

Cat on a fence _____

_____

Wild, whitewater river_____

_____

Tall, stately oak tree _____

_____

A bicycle racer _____

_____

Student at a typewriter_____

_____

Violent storm _____

_____

The perfect place to be _____

_____

Three carved figures on a table _____

_____

An unexplained bright light_____

_____

> ***Putting It Together.*** *Do I like to daydream? Do I see pictures? Hear? Feel? Smell? Do I keep my thoughts "organized?" "In control?" "Out-of-control?" Pleasant fantasies? Do I "Let go?" Direct? Enjoy? Learn? Can I see the success in just daydreaming?*

✎ Use each of the following "Daydreaming" phrases to begin a story. Each member, in turn, will add a sentence to the story until the story finishes by itself.

A huge sailing ship _____

_____

A dying man _____

_____

The deserted old house _____

_____

A strange noise outside the window _____

_____

The gentle breeze _____

_____

An old chest in the attic_____

_____

A billowy cloud _____

_____

The hidden cave _____

_____

A toy store_____

_____

The shadow in the woods _____

_____

The circus is coming _____

> ***Spin Off.*** *Go into a Think Tank. Share your daydreams and the feelings connected with them.*

MOTIVATION

> **Challenge.** *"Motivation" is the inner force that drives a person toward completion or satisfaction. Motivation must come from within; it cannot come from someone else. For example, you experience motivation when you see something you want and then put your energy into getting it.*

Explore.

✎ People frequently misuse the following words when they describe "motivation." The words, however, have basically different meanings. Give a short definition of each word, an example in your life, and how each word differs from "motivation."

Motive _____

_____

Incentive _____

_____

Direct_____

_____

Regulate _____

_____

Compel_____

_____

Compulsion_____

_____

Reward _____

_____

Control_____

_____

Overpower _____

_____

Spur _____

_____

Conduct _____

_____

Impulse _____

_____

Command _____

_____

Impel _____

_____

Putting It Together. *What really gives me energy? Fires me up? Gets me moving? Revives my engine? Stirs my soul? Who, what robs my energy? Extinguishes my fire? Stops me quick? Shuts me down?*

Spin Off. *In your Think Tank group, discuss the ways you like to learn and to be taught. Share what you don't like about learning or being taught. Form a panel of "expert learners." Share your ideas about learning and teaching.*

DESCRIBE IT GAME

> **Challenge.** *Playing a game called "Describe It," you can determine a word from clues.*

Explore.

✎ To play this game, a player attempts to describe a word by giving examples and descriptions (such as synonyms and antonyms). The class must guess the player's word.

Round I

✎ Each person gets two minutes to describe a word—someone watching the time should say when 30 seconds are left. Start out by describing the word in very general terms, but as you continue, become more precise until the word can be guessed in the last 30 seconds. No guesses are made until 90 seconds have elapsed. The best description cannot be guessed until the last 30 seconds. Each person has a turn to present a word.

WORDS YOU MAY USE	HOW TO DESCRIBE THE WORD

Round II

✎ Try to give one or two sentence descriptions so clearly that the word is guessed immediately.

WORDS YOU WILL USE	YOUR SIMPLE DEFINITION OR DESCRIPTION

> ***Putting It Together.*** *Do I like to use words to express myself? Where am I really good at it? Where do I need improvement? Why should I? Is it true that the more clearly I express myself, the more successful I appear to others? Why? When? Where? How?*
>
> ***Spin Off.*** *What are your reactions to this game. Work together with your small group to improve it. Share the revised game with the total group.*

WHERE TO PLACE THINGS

> **Challenge.** *It takes practice to improve communication with others. We are not born with communication as a gift. We develop it as a skill.*
>
> *Practice communication by giving and receiving instructions and learn by watching others struggle.*

Explore.

✎ Each team should have a set of the following designs:

2 Large squares of paper (4" x 4")	**2** Small circles (2" in diameter)
4 Small squares (2" x 2")	**4** Small rectangles (2" x 3")
4 Small triangles (2" base)	**2** Large circles (4" in diameter)
2 Large rectangles (4" x 6")	

✎ Two persons sit back to back. On the desk in front of each is an identical set of shapes. One player is a Sender, the other a silent Receiver. The Sender's task is to describe clearly what he or she is making so that the Receiver can duplicate it (without looking at the Sender's pattern). Continue this until all students have a chance to send and receive. Observers can answer the following questions:

What are common mistakes in sending? _____

_____

_____

_____

List what makes a good sender. _____

_____

_____

_____

List what makes a good receiver. _____

_____

_____

_____

> ***Putting It Together.*** *I will describe my participation as a receiver and/or sender (how involved and interested I was, not how good I was).*

✎ What did I observe about my own sending and receiving?

_____

_____

_____

_____

_____

_____

_____

> ***Spin Off.*** *Discuss with the small group what you learned about your ability to communicate clearly.*

UNIQUENESS

> ***Challenge.*** *Your "uniqueness" implies some kinds of differences when compared to "average." Where do YOU fit?*

Explore.

✎ Use the "I" statements to measure your uniqueness, and finish each sentence with your concerns in mind:

I am _____

I wish _____

I like _____

I frequently _____

I was _____

I should _____

I will _____

I want _____

I have _____

I suspect _____

I will be _____

I can _____

I would like to be _____

I rarely _____

I know _____

> ***Putting It Together.*** *I will look over my responses to these fill-ins and check three that I really like about me? Why?*
>
> ***Spin Off.*** *Assemble into your Think Tank groups. Share your responses on each incomplete sentence. Talk about your similarities and differences.*

How many of your responses were unique? _____

How many were shared by others? _____

THINK TANK PRODUCTS

> ***Challenge.*** *Your Think Tank is a small group where you can share thoughts and feelings about a specific task or problem and then proceed to develop a "product." The product can be some further research, a visual and / or audio display, a report, a newsletter, etc. In short, the product can be experienced by others.*

Explore.

✎ Use the Think Tank process to design "An Ideal Learning Situation." The process of developing a product within your Think Tank can be as follows:

1. Brainstorm in a group.
2. List your ideas in order of importance.
3. Assume responsibilities (as opposed to assigning them).
4. Let others know how the product is developing.
5. Refine the rough product.
6. Give the presentation/product.
7. Evaluate as a group or individual and provide feedback (such as satisfaction, celebration, awards, certification, etc.).

✎ Use the following chart to log your progress. (Approximately 20 minutes.)

CHECK WHEN COMPLETED	THE PROCESS	TIME LIMIT (MINUTES)	NOTES AND SUGGESTIONS
( )	1. Brainstorm ideas	3	_____
( )	2. Make choice	3	_____
( )	3. Determine course of action	3	_____
( )	4. Refine idea	3	_____
( )	5. Present idea	3	_____
( )	6. Evaluate idea's success	3	_____

> ***Spin Off.*** *Now use the Think Tank process to make a product of your choice. Use the same process and time limits. Did the process go more smoothly? Discuss any rough spots and ideas to smooth them out. Share your "Product" and "Process" with the total group*

MAKE A "SOMETHINK"

Challenge. *A "Somethink" is unique!*

Explore.

✎ Get into a group of four people. Place ONE sheet of paper between you. Your task is to make a "Somethink." You have no other instructions. Go!

✎ Watching everyone make a "Somethink," decide how each member contributed to the group. Write the name in the box that describes the efforts of that person.

Putting It Together. *How do I feel about such unclear instructions? How did I do? Who took charge? Who was bossy? Who did nothing? Too much? Who was enjoyable? Fun? Did we do OK? How could I do better? Worse? How can I tell others how to improve? How can I best compliment?*

Spin Off. *How did each person contribute to the project? Discuss your differences and similarities. What was your group's biggest problem? Have each group do it again with the other groups observing.*

✎ Fill in your own opinions of how each member did in the chart below. Then compare your opinions with the opinions of the other members of your group.

	GROUP 1	GROUP 2	GROUP 3	GROUP 4
Good Organizer				
Pleasant, Helpful				
Blocked Group Efforts				
Too Humorous				
Too Quiet				
Talked Too Much				
Blocked Progress				

HOW I SEE YOU

Challenge. *"Everybody likes me!"*

Explore.

✎ Take this page to several people who like you. Ask each person to write a short phrase saying something nice that they really feel about you. Ask them to be sincere. Avoid mixed messages and do not talk during the experience.

1.

_____

_____

2.

_____

_____

3.

_____

_____

4.

_____

_____

5.

_____

_____

6.

_____

_____

_____

7.

_____

_____

_____

8.

_____

_____

_____

> ***Putting It Together.*** *How am I after this experience?*

✎ List the following:

Three feelings _____

_____

_____

Three thoughts _____

_____

Three things I saw "new" _____

_____

_____

Three ways I am different_____

_____

_____

> ***Spin Off.*** *Share your feelings with members of your small group.*

©1991, JIST Works, Inc. • Indianapolis, Indiana

LEVELS OF IMPORTANCE

> **Challenge.** *Some things are more important to you than to others. That's the way it should be. Imagine how it would be if everything had equal importance in your life. What is really important to you?*

Explore.

✎ List 5 things that are very important to you. Then decide the most important thing. Put a "1" in front of it. Put a "2" in front of the next most important thing. Do this down to the least important ("5").

(   ) A _____

(   ) B _____

(   ) C _____

(   ) D _____

(   ) E _____

✎ List six classes you take in school. Assign levels of importance to these classes.

(   ) A _____

(   ) B _____

(   ) C _____

(   ) D _____

(   ) E _____

(   ) F _____

✎ Why is "1" so important?

_____

_____

✎ Why is "6" ***not*** as important?

_____

_____

✎ List five of your activities outside school. Assign levels of importance to these activities.

( ) A _____

( ) B _____

( ) C _____

( ) D _____

( ) E _____

> ***Putting It Together.*** *I will think of the responsibilities I have at home. I will consider the feelings I have toward others.*

✎ List five responsibilities you have at home, and, assign levels of importance to these responsibilities.

( ) A _____

( ) B _____

( ) C _____

( ) D _____

( ) E _____

✎ List five of your feelings toward others along with why you feel this way, and assign levels of importance to these feelings.

( ) A _____

( ) B _____

( ) C _____

( ) D _____

( ) E _____

> ***Spin Off.*** *Share your important things, classes, activities, responsibilities, and feelings with other members of the class in small groups. How do their ideas compare with yours? What conflicts does this cause? How do you best resolve them? Discuss issues that don't get solved easily, if at all. List possible solutions. Thank each other for sharing such important matters in your lives.*

SUCCESSFULLY UNIQUE

Challenge. *You may like to think that you communicate clearly. But the reality is that even when you say something, several messages are really being sent: 1. What you mean to say. 2. What comes out of your mouth. 3. What goes in the other person's ears. 4. What that person thinks he or she heard.*

Explore.

✎ Write a dictionary definition of "unique." (Use different dictionaries to find the meaning you like best.)

_____

_____

_____

✎ Why do you like this definition?

_____

_____

_____

✎ Rewrite the dictionary definition in your own words.

_____

_____

_____

✎ Now, research the idea of "successful."

_____

_____

_____

✎ Write a dictionary definition that you like.

_____

_____

_____

✎ Define "successful" in your own words.

_____

_____

_____

> **Putting It Together.** *I will think about people who are successful. How am I measuring their success?*

✎ I will think of a person I know and who I think is successful. What about that person makes him or her seem successful to me?

_____

_____

_____

✎ Which qualities of that person's do I think are inborn or learned (acquired)?

Inborn Qualities	Acquired Qualities
_____	_____
_____	_____
_____	_____

✎ Three of my qualities that are inborn and three that are acquired.

Inborn Qualities	Acquired Qualities
_____	_____
_____	_____
_____	_____

> **Spin Off.** *Now, do your best to communicate your inborn and acquired qualities to others in your group. Be aware that the message may not be heard and understood as you intended. Listen closely as other members attempt to communicate clearly.*

A SUCCESSFUL PERSON I KNOW

Challenge. *Success is an attitude that works well. An attitude is a state of mind or mood. Moods are something people experience.*

Could it be true that a "Successful Person" is one who often has a mood that works well for that person? Determine the qualities that make up a successful person.

Explore.

✎ Write the first name of a person that you feel is successful.

_____

✎ List three specific "successful" things that person does.
Example: Runs an outboard repair shop well enough to make a living and do the things he wants to do in life.

    1. _____

    2. _____

    3. _____

✎ Write what you think that person's overall mood or attitude is.

_____

_____

_____

_____

✎ Define "successful" using your dictionary.

_____

_____

_____

_____

Putting It Together. *Why do I like that person's success? What does that tell me about myself?*

Spin Off. *Share the successful people patterns with your small group. Tell why you like that person's success.*

WAYS THAT I AM ALREADY SUCCESSFUL

> ***Challenge.*** *Say the following phrases to yourself.*
>
> *"I am beginning to sense that success is not something that I achieve (after much hard work at some future day).*
>
> *"I am now sure that "being successful" is simply accepting the progress I have already made and who I already am—at this moment.*
>
> *"I now assume the attitude of being successful."*
>
> *Look at your own successes. Determine what some of them are.*

Explore.

✎ List three things that you DO (with hands, brain, body) well.

1. _____

_____

2. _____

_____

3. _____

_____

> ***Putting It Together.*** *What makes me special?*

✎ Three ways I AM that make me a special person.

1. _____

_____

2. _____

_____

3. _____

_____

✎ Three qualities I already have as a friend:

1. _____

_____

2. _____

_____

3. _____

_____

✎ Use the answers to the statements above to check the appropriate boxes in the chart below.

	LOW	MEDIUM	HIGH
Skills			
Personality			
Friendship			

Spin Off. *Share with your group some ways your life is already successful.*

SEEDS OF SERVICE

> **Challenge.** *You may have one of two attitudes:*
> *A. Get-what-you-can*
> *B. Give-what-you-are-able*
> *Rather than thinking of ways to make money, I will create ways to give—to be of service to others.*

Explore.

✎ Use the "personal brainstorming" technique. Jot down ideas about how you can serve others by giving of yourself. Write as fast as you get the ideas even if some don't look practical. Don't try to evaluate or critique your ideas.

_____

_____

_____

_____

_____

_____

_____

_____

_____

_____

_____

_____

_____

_____

_____

_____

> **Spin Off.** *That's all there is to it. You have entered these seeds into your consciousness. You can act on the important ones whenever you need them.*

PLANNING AND SCHEDULING

> **Challenge.** *You have valuable gifts to give—your time and energy. You can spend lots of time using little energy (like sitting in a boring lecture). Or you can take a short time expending much energy (like sports or an intense game).*

Explore.

✎ Use the technique of "personal brainstorming" to name ways you expend energy. Record your thoughts as fast as they enter your mind. Don't try to evaluate or critique what you write.

_____

_____

_____

_____

_____

_____

_____

_____

_____

_____

_____

_____

_____

_____

_____

_____

_____

_____

_____

_____

_____

✎ Write specific places or ways you expend only a little bit of energy:

_____

_____

_____

_____

_____

_____

_____

_____

_____

_____

_____

_____

_____

_____

_____

_____

_____

_____

_____

_____

_____

_____

> ***Putting It Together.*** *Who wants more of my time and energy than I want to give? What do they want of me? Why? Is it the way they go about it or what they want? How can I help them ask me differently? How can I let them know they expect the wrong things? What do I expect out of others in my life (I will think of the main people)? Am I realistic? Do I allow them to make mistakes? Be human? How can I change my expectations? Am I open to change?*
>
> ***Spin Off.*** *Meet with your small group to discuss plans for helping you avoid conflicts with others who demand your time and energy.*

NEEDS

> **Challenge.** *A NEED is a necessity, something useful or required. Or a need can be a lack of something you want.*

Explore.

✎ Start to define your needs by filling out the chart below.

NEED	CIRCLE LEVEL OF NEED	HOW BEST TO MEET THIS NEED
Acceptance	Low High	
Self-Worth	Low High	
Freedom to Explore	Low High	

✎ Decide two other needs you have.

NEED	CIRCLE LEVEL OF NEED	HOW BEST TO MEET THIS NEED
	Low High	
	Low High	

> **Putting It Together.** *How are the needs of others the same or different from my own? What words will I use to describe these needs?*

✎ Find two ways the needs of others are different from your own:

1. _____

2. _____

✎ Find two ways the needs of others are the same as your own:

1. _____

2. _____

✎ In your small groups, work together to define the following terms:

Necessity_____

_____

Desire_____

_____

Lack _____

_____

Want _____

_____

Spin Off. *Discuss these terms, using examples from your own life. What does the following saying mean? "He's not poor who has little, only he who drinks too much?"*

FEELINGS DEFINED

Explore.

✎ Write eight words that describe the good feelings you have at times. Describe these feelings in detail. Use your dictionary and thesaurus to get a better idea of each definition. Then write your own definition. Give an example of when these feelings occurred in your life.

MY FEELING	DEFINITION AND EXAMPLE
1.	
2.	
3.	
4.	
5.	
6.	
7.	
8.	

Putting It Together. How do I feel having a day made up of good feelings? Who does it happens to? How can I make it happen?

Spin Off. Meet with small groups to discuss your nice feelings and how to get them.

DISCARDED COMPUTER PARTS

> **Challenge.** *According to Roget's Thesaurus, "Useless" can be defined in any number of ways including "rubbishy," "trashy," "junky," "rubble," "scrap," "waste," "chaff," "jetsam," "litter," "fruitless," "inept," "unproductive," and "unfunctional."*
>
> *What can be seen by some as "useless," can be experienced by others as "useful." Consider the scenario below as an example.*

Explore.

✎ You are an electronic computer part that was just tossed into the throw-away pile.

What part are you? _____

_____

Why were you discarded? _____

_____

Who put you here? _____

_____

Tell why you should be recycled. _____

_____

> **Putting It Together.** *How can I become useful again. What will it take? How do I go about it?*

✎ I will describe a recycling process that will make me a valuable part again.

_____

_____

_____

_____

_____

> **Spin Off.** *Discuss with your group the feeling of not fitting in and being useful. Share ways to get the useful feeling back.*

MY PROBLEM

> ***Challenge.*** *Finding solutions to problems takes thoughtful consideration.*

Explore.

✎ List six problems that other people have.

1. _____   4. _____

2. _____   5. _____

3. _____   6. _____

✎ List four possible causes for problems.

1. _____   3. _____

2. _____   4. _____

> ***Putting It Together.*** *What problems do I have in my life? How do they affect my life? What are some possible causes? How can I handle them effectively?*
>
> ***Spin Off.*** *Discuss within your group problems people have, how it interferes with their lives, some possible causes, and what they can do about them (inappropriate and successful approaches).*

✎ Decide as a group a specific "Life" problem. Identify the "Roles." Assign these "Roles" to members of the group. Within character, discuss the problem and possible solutions. Share the findings with the total group.

The Problem: _____

_____

The Roles:

_____   _____

_____   _____

_____   _____

CONTRACTING

> **Challenge.** *A contract is an agreement between two or more persons TO DO something or TO BE a certain way. You can contract to perform a service or produce a product. This is done in an agreed upon way for a specified reward or compensation.*

Explore.

✎ You will be contracting to do task(s) for an agreed upon reward (grade? extra credits? etc.). You, as the contractor, and the instructor/facilitator sign and date the contract when you both agree on the tasks and rewards.

INITIALS OF INSTRUCTOR	POSSIBLE TASKS	COMPENSATION
( )	Research 10 words that relate to being successful.	
( )	Make a test of "Being Successful," matching 20 words in the left column with definitions or examples in the right column.	
( )	Write two, single-page biographies of successful people.	
( )	Draw and explain a famous invention.	
( )	Write a five-minute script about a successful attitude.	
( )	Write a two-page account of your typical successful day from start to finish.	
( )	Arrange for a successful person to speak to your class.	
( )	Create a puppet show, play, or skit describing success.	
( )	Make a complete bibliography of success-related materials.	

INITIALS OF INSTRUCTOR	POSSIBLE TASKS	COMPENSATION
( )	Make and teach a 10-minute teaching unit on the topic of success with pre- and post-tests.	
( )	Make a five-minute audio-visual presentation on poor attitudes.	
( )	Other project(s) of your choice:	
( )		
( )		
( )		

DATED	SIGNED	
_____	Contractor _____	
	Instructor/Facilitator	

✎ Make an appointment with the instructor/facilitator to contract for your task(s) and the compensation expected.

> ***Putting It Together.*** *Have I done my best to decide a task and contract for the reward? What have I learned about how I "sell" myself and how I "push" for a fair compensation?*
>
> ***Spin Off.*** *Share the experiences of the small group with the total group.*

BURIED TALENTS

> ***Challenge.*** *An employer gave two employees $2,000 each with the instruction to "use it wisely until I return." One employee provided a service to people and realized a fair profit. The other fearfully buried the money until the boss returned. Which employee used the money wisely? Determine ways you can make money by uncovering your buried talents.*

Explore.

✎ Your task is to take $10 and turn it into $50 in three months or less. Your method will be to provide a service or a product to the world (those around you, your classmates, your family, or your neighbors). Your dollars will grow when you receive a fair profit for the energy you expend in your service or product. For a product, you may wish to buy something and sell it for a profit. Or you may buy and gradually "trade up," then sell. For a service, use the "personal brainstorming" exercise that follows.

✎ 10 ways I can increase my service to the world.

1._____
2._____
3._____
4._____
5._____
6._____
7._____
8._____
9._____
10._____

✎ Rank the best three ideas.

First: _____

Second: _____

Third:_____

✎ Use your first choice to write a plan to begin ASAP ("As Soon As Possible").

_____

_____

_____

_____

✎ Use a separate sheet for alternative plans for your second and third ideas.

✎ Keep exact records (to the penny). Do not spend—invest! After you achieve $50, give yourself a percentage of the profit. Reinvest the rest. Write "Service to the World" on your books, posters, bumper- stickers—think SERVICE, not profit! Report your plans, progress, and profits to your instructor/contractor. Providing a service to the world will automatically bring a reward. The "payoffs" may be personal satisfaction rather than financial rewards.

> ***Putting It Together.*** *Do I really believe that I "get" when I "give?" What are my gut-level feelings about being of "service to the world?"*
>
> ***Spin Off.*** *With your small group, tally your efforts at investment. Each member can encourage you to continue to modify your plan.*

INTELLIGENCE

Challenge. *Research the concept of "intelligence."*

Explore.

✎ What is intelligence?

_____

_____

_____

✎ List three ways intelligence is tested.

1._____

2._____

3._____

✎ Being creative is to be inventive or productive. List five ways you have been creative.

1._____

2._____

3._____

4._____

5._____

Putting It Together. *I will think of ways I am creative. In what ways have I been inventive and productive?*

✎ I will list three specific "creations" of mine that I like.

1._____

2._____

3._____

Spin Off. *Meet with your group to make your own personal list of ways you have already demonstrated your "smarts" in this class. Then appoint a representative to convince the instructor of your main points (as the whole group listens respectfully).*

IT'S YOUR CHOICE

Challenge. *Your career choices are yours—either by your own decisions or by leaving the choice to someone else.*

Explore.

✎ Circle if you agree or disagree. Explain your answer.

DECISION	CHOICE
Many people are concerned about my best interest. _____ _____	Agree Disagree
People with special skills are more likely to be employed. _____ _____	Agree Disagree
The people helping me to pick my course of study know what is best for me. _____ _____	Agree Disagree
The more I put into my education, the better education I get. _____ _____	Agree Disagree
The more years of schooling I have, the more successful I will be in life. _____ _____	Agree Disagree

Putting It Together. *How many of my educational choices do I usually make for myself? Did I choose my own classes? Do I have adequate skills to do it well?*

Spin Off. *Share your feelings about personal choices with your small group, and "hear" new ideas about choices.*

DO YOU AGREE?

Challenge. *Everyone has an opinion about what is right and wrong. This is your chance to offer some of your own opinions.*

Explore.

✎ Read each statement. Decide if you agree or disagree with each one. Circle the appropriate response. Put an "X" in front of the ones you strongly agree or strongly disagree with.

	STATEMENT	CHOICE	
___	Always show trust and confidence.	Agree	Disagree
___	If you are right, you don't have to see the other person's side.	Agree	Disagree
___	Always be fair and just.	Agree	Disagree
___	It's OK to compare one person with another.	Agree	Disagree
___	People change faster for friends than for family.	Agree	Disagree
___	Keep rules simple and few.	Agree	Disagree
___	Keep problems to yourself. Don't let outsiders in.	Agree	Disagree
___	Be kind and courteous.	Agree	Disagree
___	There is no "democracy" — someone is always in charge.	Agree	Disagree
___	The whole family should suffer if someone is angry or down.	Agree	Disagree
___	Satisfy your own needs first.	Agree	Disagree
___	Don't plan anything so you won't be disappointed.	Agree	Disagree
___	Never say harsh or unkind words.	Agree	Disagree
___	Never show anger or dislike.	Agree	Disagree
___	My goal is to be perfect.	Agree	Disagree

Putting It Together. *What two of these opinions do I feel the strongest about? Which two opinions are not important to me?*

Spin Off. *Read each statement in your small group and discuss. Try to get 100 percent agreement. Discuss why you can't always get complete agreement.*

TEST ME

> ***Challenge.*** *Test results can be helpful. In the lower grades, test results help teachers place you in suitable classes. Test results also helped to monitor your progress in the different subjects. More importantly, test results can help YOU make YOUR OWN CHOICES of classes and training courses.*

Explore.

✎ Get the results of two tests you have taken in the last year—one academic and one personal interest test. Describe what you learned about yourself from these tests.

    1. _____

    2. _____

Test 1 (Academic):

✎ What you learned about yourself:

_____

_____

✎ How this helps your career choice:

_____

_____

_____

Test 2 (Interest):

✎ What you learned about yourself:

_____

_____

> ***Putting It Together.*** *What have I learned about myself from tests? Do tests really tell me whether I am successful?*
>
> ***Spin Off.*** *Share ways to get information from your school files that you can use for your benefit (for example, job applications and school applications). Share what you learned about yourself with the small group.*

SIMULATION I: *The Game*

> **Challenge.** *You have completed the activities of Section I, "You Are Unique." Now put what you have learned about yourself to work in* **SIMULATION I: The Game.**

Explore.

✎ A major game company has just challenged your own small group to develop a challenging, high-quality language game that can relax and amuse young adults as it teaches them to communicate enjoyably and with satisfaction.

The company has guidelines to follow. *The Game* must be:

    A. Stimulating and enjoyable
    B. Organized with clear directions
    C. Of marketable quality
    D. Instructive, but not "stuffy"
    E. Non-competitive—everyone "wins," nobody "loses"

✎ Use your Think Tank group to develop your characters, game board design (or computer screen), directions, manipulation devices, color scheme, etc. "Personally brainstorm" how to begin developing *The Game*.

_____

_____

_____

_____

_____

_____

_____

_____

_____

_____

_____

> **Spin Off.** *Present your first rough ideas for the game to your team. Come to an agreement about the product. Make The Game! Play it!*

©1991, JIST Works, Inc. • Indianapolis, Indiana

EVALUATION OF *THE GAME*

Challenge. *Evaluate your new product.*

Explore.

✎ After you play *The Game* for the first time, indicate what you think about your product:

CHARACTERISTIC	LOW				HIGH
Stimulating and enjoyable	1	2	3	4	5
Incentive for finishing	1	2	3	4	5
Instructional	1	2	3	4	5
Organized	1	2	3	4	5
Targeted age and group	1	2	3	4	5
Marketable product	1	2	3	4	5
Originality	1	2	3	4	5
Other _____	1	2	3	4	5
_____	1	2	3	4	5

✎ List problems and solutions with the first draft of *The Game:*

_____

_____

_____

_____

_____

_____

Spin Off. *Revise and evaluate your game as many times as needed. Have others play and evaluate your game.*

SMALL GROUP INVENTORY I

Challenge. *Evaluate your small group.*

Explore.

✎ Now that you have completed the first simulation in this book, express your opinions about the small group you have been working with. Think carefully how your group worked together. Work individually.

CHARACTERISTIC	CIRCLE ONE		
	LOW	AVG	HIGH
Level of Sincerity			
Your desire to do your best	1	2	3
Your attempt to learn more	1	2	3
Comments:			
Research			
Use of many sources	1	2	3
Clear, straight-forward sharing of material	1	2	3
Comments:			
Awareness			
Your attempt to listen to the ideas of others	1	2	3
Level at which the group communicates ideas	1	2	3
Comments:			
Cooperation			
Level at which you work together	1	2	3
Understanding of needs of others	1	2	3
Comments:			
Product			
Completion of work	1	2	3
Clarity of work	1	2	3
Appearance of work	1	2	3
Comments:			
Your Overall Satisfaction With the Group	1	2	3
Comments:			

SELF-INVENTORY I

> **Challenge.** *Evaluate yourself. How are you doing so far? Before you begin answering these questions, review your responses in Section I and what you have learned about yourself.*

Explore.

✎ Ask yourself these questions honestly and with a fair degree of self-examination.

CHARACTERISTIC	CIRCLE ONE		
	LOW	AVG	HIGH
My Level of Sincerity			
Desire to do my best	1	2	3
Attempt to learn more	1	2	3
Wish to cooperate	1	2	3
My Research			
Use of many sources	1	2	3
Clear, straight-forward responses in book	1	2	3
Attempt to find more resources	1	2	3
My Awareness of Self			
Discovering new things	1	2	3
Desire to improve	1	2	3
Working on personal challenges	1	2	3
My Awareness of Others		+	
Cooperation in groups and Think Tanks	1	2	3
Level of ability to communicate ideas	1	2	3
Ability to assist others	1	2	3
My Written and Oral Product			
Quality of oral report	1	2	3
Excellence of written work	1	2	3
Amount of preparation for oral or written work	1	2	3
The Carry-over Outside School			
Homework	1	2	3
Degree of interest in my studies	1	2	3
Hobbies and interests that relate	1	2	3
Overall Sense of Personal Satisfaction			
My satisfaction in my personal growth	1	2	3
Ability to be a friend increasingly	1	2	3
More awareness of the world	1	2	3
Amount of available energy used	1	2	3
Degree I progressed compared to my potential	1	2	3

MOVING ON

After completing the first section of this book, you now know more about yourself.

You should start seeing that you are ALREADY a success. This first section of the book and its game simulation have shown you your own "uniqueness."

In Section II, "Success with Others," you will see how successful you already are with those around you. You may be surprised to find out that the members of your small group already see you as successful. As you experience the next section of this book, you will find your success as seen through the eyes of others.

Don't forget, there are no "right" or "wrong" answers, only differences of opinion.

SECTION II
Success With Others

"Being successful" is sharing your ideas and feelings with others. The people you work with in Section II understand themselves as unique, just as you have. Those people will learn to understand why you are unique. And, as you express yourself, you will discover your similarities.

The key to "being successful" is realizing you are NOW a successful person. You are successful not because of WHO you are or WHAT you accomplish, you are successful because you are planning, attempting, doing, and being. Success is not far away in the future. Success is an attitude you can learn and start to practice right now. At some point, you may find yourself saying, "Hey, this man Hooker is right! I am already successful!"

In Section I, you focused on discovering your own unique self. You explored what you think is important in your life. You revealed your feelings and studied your ability to learn. In short, you saw yourself as unique.

In Section II, you will focus on the people around you. Working with your group, you interview others, discuss, evaluate, and make decisions. You and others will share feelings and reactions, first in small Think Tank groups and then in your large group. What makes this section interesting is that everyone else has worked through the self-inquiries in Section I.

You begin this section by learning how to question people in an interview. You study their interests and attitudes, rather than your own. This is the first step in learning to work successfully with others. Many activities follow that ask you to consider what the other people in your group think and feel.

In this section, you work together towards the simulation, *Our Business*. This simulation draws on the full knowledge and creativity of the game team you put together for your first simulation.

INTERVIEWING TECHNIQUE

> **Challenge.** *Interviewing others is enjoyable if you first determine the basic questions to ask. Good questions relate to the interests of the person you interview. For example, you would not ask an eye doctor about foot care.*

Explore.

✎ Pick a classmate to interview. Make a list of questions to ask that person (for example, the person's history, likes, dislikes, activities, hobbies, school, family, etc.). Keep your questions related to a central topic, being as specific as possible. But allow for interesting sidetracks (example: "What nice memories do you have of being five years old?").

_____

_____

_____

_____

_____

✎ Brainstorm the following problem: "Questions to ask in an interview with the janitor about a school maintenance problem."

_____

_____

_____

_____

✎ Brainstorm a list of interview questions to ask your principal, guidance counselor, teacher, or other interesting people. Trim your list and write the best questions below in the order they will be asked. Use extra paper if necessary.

Principal

_____

_____

_____

_____

_____

 ©1991, JIST Works, Inc. • Indianapolis, Indiana

Guidance Counselor

_____
_____
_____
_____
_____

Teacher

_____
_____
_____
_____
_____

Another Adult

_____
_____
_____
_____
_____

Putting It Together. *How did I do? Did I ask the right questions? How could I have done better? Was I an effective interviewer? Why or Why not?*

Spin Off. *Now, interview the persons you have chosen. Work in teams of two or three if possible. After the interview, discuss the information you learned. Did you ask the right questions? What did you learn about others? About yourself?*

PLANNING A JOB INTERVIEW

> **Challenge.** *Job Interviews can be crucial as you seek employment. It is usually the first and only chance you have to make the proper impression.*

Explore.

✎ Assemble into Think Tanks. Brainstorm "Do's" and "Don'ts" for a job interview. Use the following list to assist you.

Leadership	Maturity	Appearance	Manners
Intelligence	Attitude	Posture	Punctuality
Alertness	Enthusiasm	Poise	Speech
Personality	Education	Originality	Sincerity
Training	Experience		

✎ List Do's as a job applicant:

_____

_____

_____

_____

_____

_____

_____

_____

_____

_____

_____

_____

_____

_____

_____

_____

_____

_____

_____

_____

✎ List Don'ts as a job applicant:

_____

_____

_____

_____

_____

_____

_____

_____

_____

_____

_____

_____

_____

_____

_____

_____

_____

_____

_____

> ***Putting It Together.*** *For what job, would I like to be interviewed? What are my strengths? Interests? Aptitudes? Training? Hobbies? How will this help me get the job?*
>
> ***Spin Off.*** *Use your list of Do's and Don'ts to act out job interviews. Before the small group begins, decide the job you are interviewing for so the questions will be specific. Each person can roleplay as an applicant. The others can be a committee interviewing the applicant for a job. After you are interviewed, ask the committee to give you suggestions for a better interview.*
>
> *You may then share ways the committee could have improved the interview.*

INTERVIEWING

> ***Challenge.*** *I was talking to my candle-making friend when a famous movie actress walked into the candle shop. I wanted to talk to the star—so I did. She was a person just like me and was just as fascinated that I wanted to talk with her as I was interested in talking to her.*

Explore.

✎ Use the dictionary to discover the meanings for the following terms. Think how you can weave these ideas into your interviewing style.

Recording/note taking _____

_____

Respect _____

_____

Ease _____

_____

Flow _____

_____

Tone _____

_____

Direction _____

_____

✎ Pick one of the following people to interview:

Family Member	Politician	Crafts Person
Recreation Leader	Neighbor	Business Person
Environmentalist	Social Security Recipient	Other_____

✎ Write down possible questions to ask this person. Arrange the questions in the order you want to ask. Which question do you want to ask first? Which question do you want to ask next? What information is the most important to you?

____ A _____

____ B _____

____ C _____

____ D _____

____ E _____

____ F _____

____ G _____

____ H _____

____ I _____

____ J _____

____ K _____

____ L _____

____ M _____

____ N _____

____ O _____

____ P _____

Putting It Together. *Before the interview — Am I prepared? Not too tense? Not too relaxed? Am I too self-conscious? Do I really want to know that person better? Will I help them be their best?*

After the interview — Was I prepared? Tense? Relaxed? Not self-conscious? Do I know that person better? Do I want to share this with others? Would I like to do this some more?

Spin Off. *Share your interview with your small group. Did your questions get the responses you wanted? Discuss ways that you can make your questions better. Tell the large group about the person you interviewed.*

WORKING TOGETHER

Challenge. *To "cooperate" means to do a task together. Many jobs are done best by a team that works in harmony. Each role is important to complete the product.*

Explore.

✎ Divide into groups of three to five. The teacher or group leader will tear a large sheet of paper into as many odd-shaped pieces as there are members. After the pieces are torn, the teacher should place a small square of adhesive tape on one side of each of the puzzle pieces.

✎ The small group gathers around three sides of a table in front of the class. Now comes the hard part—the members are each blindfolded! After the blindfolds are in place, the teacher gives each person a part of the puzzle. Each person, one at a time, must describe the puzzle piece by feeling its shape, the location of the tape, and the torn and smooth edges. If each person describes the puzzle piece accurately, the team should be able to put the puzzle together on the table.

✎ Your task, as observers, is to evaluate how well each group works together. Use the following form to make notes.

	WHO TOOK LEADERSHIP? DESCRIBE	WHO FOLLOWED WELL? DESCRIBE	WHO NEEDED HELP IN COOPERATION? TELL HOW	HOW I WOULD DO IT BETTER
Group I				
Group II				
Group III				
Group IV				

COOPERATION

> ***Challenge.*** *Cooperation is useful when two or more people are making decisions. Your opinions and ideas are essential.*

Explore.

✎ What is "cooperation?" Define the word and give examples.

_____

_____

✎ List three characteristics of cooperative people.

1. _____

2. _____

3. _____

✎ List three characteristics of uncooperative people.

1. _____

2. _____

3. _____

✎ Look up the term "co-op." Give an example of such an enterprise.

_____

_____

✎ Define "corporation." How does that word relate to the word "cooperate?"

_____

_____

> ***Putting It Together.*** *Am I cooperative? When is it easy to cooperate? Hard? With whom? Why? Am I doing better since I feel my "successful" attitude? Do members of my small group cooperate? What can I do better? How can I get worse?*
>
> ***Spin Off.*** *Think about the cooperative puzzle-solving project you just completed. Did you think you had good directions? Could you finish the puzzle easily?*

✎ Looking at the previous page, copy your definition of "cooperation."

_____

_____

✎ Describe four times when cooperation was important in your life.

1._____

2._____

3._____

4._____

Putting It Together. *What are four times when I decided to do things differently from what the group was doing at the time. Did other people think I was uncooperative? Why?*

Spin Off. *Assemble into small groups. Within each group, discuss the idea of selling a new line of refrigerators to Arctic explorers. (Act out such a scene.) The committee cannot agree. How can this problem be resolved? Notice your own cooperation. Does cooperation mean "giving up?" Explain why you feel this way.*

How can you convince the committee to use your own answer to the problem? Share your thinking with the total group. Thank each other.

EFFECTIVE "FOLLOWERSHIP"

> ***Challenge.*** *Being a good follower is just as important as being a good leader.*

Explore.

✎ List three ways you acted as a "follower" in the exercises "Cooperation" and "Working Together."

1. _____

_____

2. _____

_____

3. _____

_____

✎ Was your decision always a part of the final choice? _____

✎ How did that make you feel? Explain:

_____

_____

_____

_____

_____

_____

_____

✎ Think of three other members of the group and tell how you think they felt like a "follower."

1. _____

_____

2. _____

_____

3. _____

_____

✎ List three situations where you were glad to be a follower. Explain why:

1. _____

2. _____

3. _____

✎ How is being a follower and a leader different or similar?

Different? _____

_____

Similar? _____

_____

> ***Putting It Together.*** *How do I like being told what to do? Who does it best? How? When? Where? Why? Some people irritate me when they tell me what to do. Who? Why? How could they do it differently? Do I have a right to tell them? How? When? I'm somebody else's "pain in the lower back." Whose? What do I do? How could I do it differently?*
>
> ***Spin Off.*** *Share with your small group your thoughts and feelings about being a follower. A leader. Neither! Do a role playing skit about good leadership and followership. Share with the total group.*

YOU ARE THE BOSS

> **Challenge.** *You are the boss of a large clothing company. There are two job openings: one in the shipping department and one in the computer room. Eight people are applying for these two jobs.*

Explore.

✎ The instructor will show you eight photos of people applying for a job. Who would you choose? You must circle L ("like") if you like the applicant at first glance or circle DL ("dislike") if you don't like the applicant.

APPLICANT'S NAME	DECISION	APPLICANT'S NAME	DECISION
1._____	L DL	5._____	L DL
2._____	L DL	6._____	L DL
3._____	L DL	7._____	L DL
4._____	L DL	8._____	L DL

✎ Look at each applicant's picture again. Tell one or two qualities you like or dislike about each person.

1. _____

2. _____

3. _____

4. _____

5. _____

6. _____

7. _____

8. _____

✎ Decide the one you would hire for the following jobs. Tell why you picked each applicant for that department.

Shipping Department: (Applicant's Number) _____

Why you would hire this person? _____

_____

Computer Room: (Applicant's Number) _____

Why you would hire this person? _____

_____

Putting It Together. *I just had to judge some people based on their looks only. How did I feel about that? What turned me against some? Eyes? Mouth? Expression? Age? Gender? Am I judged by my looks? What do my eyes "say?" Mouth? Expression? Posture? How do I want people to judge me?*

Spin Off. *Discuss these issues: Do you ever decide about a person by appearance only? Do you think you can recognize someone who is honest? Could you tell someone you should stay away from by appearance alone? Plan a better way to evaluate others for these jobs. Share yours with the total group.*

TEAM EVALUATION OF PROSPECTIVE EMPLOYEES

> ***Challenge.*** *Your team is a company that must expand.*
> *Determine, as a team, the two new positions in your company*
> *and develop a complete, written job description of each position.*

Explore.

✎ Each member brings two pictures of ordinary people (from magazines, newspapers, or wallet). One member shows one photo and briefly describes the person. The team's task is to decide whether or not to hire that person for the specific job opening you have. Each member should write his or her personal reasons (pro and con) and later share them.

Job Opening A

Title:_____

Duties and Responsibilities:_____

_____

_____

_____

APPLICANT #	(CIRCLE ONE) HIRE?		GIVE YOUR REASONS
1	Yes	No	_____
2	Yes	No	_____
3	Yes	No	_____
4	Yes	No	_____
5	Yes	No	_____
6	Yes	No	_____
7	Yes	No	_____
8	Yes	No	

Job Opening B

Title:_____

Duties and Responsibilities:_____

_____

_____

APPLICANT #	(CIRCLE ONE) HIRE?		GIVE YOUR REASONS
1	Yes	No	_____
2	Yes	No	_____
3	Yes	No	_____
4	Yes	No	_____
5	Yes	No	_____
6	Yes	No	_____
7	Yes	No	_____
8	Yes	No	

Putting It Together. What qualities do bosses want? Do I have them? What makes me already successful — even if I don't have the special job training for some jobs? What is my attitude?

When have I been judged poorly? What did I do? Should I do anything about the judgment? Could I have done it differently? Was it their misjudgment?

Spin Off. Compare and discuss your decisions about each applicant. Are first judgments ever wrong? When? Why? How? What can you tell from a face? Body? Clothes? Hair? Is it fair to judge a person at first glance? Second glance? Why do it? What is an "attitude?" What attitudes do employers want? What attitudes do employees want? What happened when you try convince the others to hire an applicant you liked but they didn't?

DISCUSSIONS AND DEBATES

> ***Challenge.*** *There are formal procedures that you can follow for presenting opinions and ideas to groups. Some of these formal methods are questioning experts, pro-con debates, and presentation / feedback. These methods use a logical, democratic, and interesting format.*

Explore.

Expert(s) Questioning

✎ In "expert questioning," you seek information by asking questions of an expert. Many questions are prepared in advance to ensure a smoother flow of information.

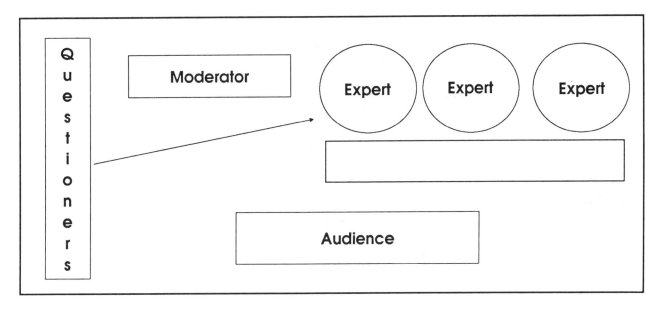

✎ Your small group will divide into the following roles to demonstrate this method of presentation to the total group.

Questioners: _____

_____

Experts: _____

_____

Moderator: _____

_____

✎ You will be asked about your special hobby or interest. Remember that if you talk about something you enjoy, your attitude will make the presentation interesting. If you don't know an answer, say so without embarrassment.

List a special hobby or interest that you consider yourself an expert:

_____

Pro-Con Debate

✎ In a pro-con debate, differing sides of the same issue are represented by experts. Someone may take an opposing view to provide interest in the discussion and to learn about the opposing view.

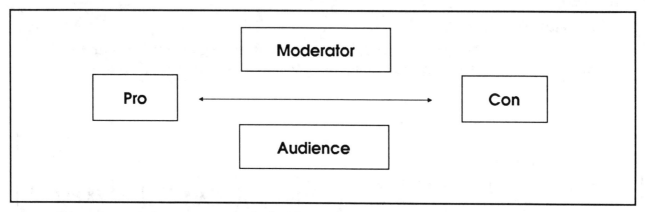

State an opinion you strongly hold: _____

_____

✎ Again, assume roles and present your opinion to the total group.

Presentation/Feedback

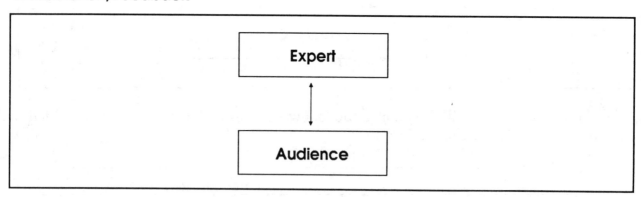

✎ One expert talks to the audience and then answers questions from that audience.

What is your area of interest that you can describe to the class? _____

_____

✎ Make an "expert" presentation to the total group.

✎ Pick three presentations to evaluate from I, II, and III.

EVALUATE THREE PRESENTATIONS	I EXPERTS QUESTIONING			II PRO-CON PANELS DEBATE			III PRESENTATION FEEDBACK		
	A	B	C	A	B	C	A	B	C
Were the arguments convincing?									
Did they research the topic adequately?									
Did they include pertinent aspects of the topic?									
Was the team well organized?									
Did they listen to the opposing sides' argument?									
What was the overall impression of the presentation?									
Offer some suggestions for improvement:									

Comments:

Presentations A: _____

_____

_____

_____

Presentations B: _____

_____

_____

_____

Presentations C: _____

_____

_____

_____

VOTE FOR IT

> **Challenge.** *You often make group decisions by voting for or against an issue. A decision you make involves one vote. If you and another person must decide an issue, there are two votes. The outcome could be two pro's (for), two con's (against), or one for and one against the issue.*

Explore.

✎ Define and try to give examples of the following voting terms:

Compromise: _____

_____

Alternative: _____

_____

Majority: _____

_____

Minority: _____

_____

Persuasion: _____

_____

Filibuster: _____

_____

✎ You can arrive at group decisions several ways. Give an example of each of the following terms and where it may be used.

Secret ballot: _____

Open ballot: _____

Roll call: _____

Consensus: _____

Opinion survey: _____

Others (list): _____

> **Spin Off.** *Assemble your Think Tank to devise a ballot that requires the decision of the whole class.*

✎ Think of three different issues to vote on.

BALLOT
Issue #1 _____

_____

Issue #2 _____

_____

Issue #3 _____

_____

OUTCOME		
	# Of Votes	% Of Votes
Issue #1		
Issue #2		
Issue #3		

✎ What percentage of votes is required to win? Does it differ with issues or people? From place to place? Discuss the differences.

_____

_____

_____

_____

_____

_____

_____

_____

_____

BE AN EXPERT

> **Challenge.** *An expert "doubletalker" was hired to fool the professionals at a recent national conference. He knew nothing about his topic but could invent words and concepts and talk for hours. The audience rated him as the best and most knowledgeable speaker of the conference.*
>
> *You may be a "doubletalking" expert. It takes more than just brains—it takes nerve!*

Explore.

✎ Be bold! Pick a subject you know nothing about, and then be specific! For example, don't merely talk about "space." Give your topic as "The Function of Columbia's Inertial Guidance System on Suborbital Flights." Write your specific "expert" subject here:

_____

✎ Each of you have three minutes to be an expert in front of the class. You will give a short introduction and answer questions from the audience. Give "expert" answers, even if you don't know what you are talking about. Make up answers, words, and ideas. Convince the class you know what you are talking about. (Oh, yes, I almost forgot... You will be given your topic by a classmate as you get to the front of the room. The topic you picked is to be given to someone else.) Keep in mind an old adage: "Prepare for 10 hours to speak well for 10 minutes. Prepare for 10 minutes to speak poorly for 10 hours."

> **Putting It Together.** *I'm being asked to give "baloney" to others. Why would an exercise in "expert" want me to practice this stuff? Value? What is honesty? Integrity? Believability? Who uses doubletalk and makes a living at it? Does that bother me?*
>
> **Spin Off.** *Evaluate your success at being an "expert," off-the-cuff, speaker.*

EVALUATING EXPERTS: YOUR CHALLENGE

> ***Challenge.*** *"X" means "unknown," a "spirt" is a drip under pressure. Thus, an "X-spirt" is "an unknown drip under pressure."*

Explore.

✎ Name three persons in your groups who were good at "experting." What were their expert qualities?

PERSON	THEIR "EXPERT" QUALITIES
1.	
2.	
3.	

✎ What do you know most about? (Don't be humble or shy!) What do you feel really tuned into, have studied, or found the most interesting? Be specific.

_____

_____

_____

_____

✎ Do you want to learn more or spend time doing this? Yes_____ No_____

Why? _____

_____

✎ Write some ideas on how you can put more time or energy into what you are interested in:

_____

_____

_____

_____

✎ Do others know about these interests? Yes_____ No_____

Who? _____

_____

✎ Who else knows enough to help you in this area of "expertise?"

_____

_____

✎ How can they help? Be specific.

_____

_____

_____

Putting It Together. *Do I like letting others know what I am good at? Why? When? Do I do it enough? What is my usual method of gaining respect? Does it work for me? Where can I improve on my presentation of myself? What can I do to become even more of an "expert" in my chosen interest? What can I ask of others to assist me in my quest for knowledge and proficiency? What IS proficiency?*

Spin Off. *Share your interests with others in your small group. Get some ideas on how to make your proficiency better known . Tell some ideas for others. What about "blowing your own horn?" Role play a skit of experts using different means to tell of their skills and expertise.*

©1991, JIST Works, Inc. • Indianapolis, Indiana

THE DECISION-MAKING PROCESS

Challenge. *I (the author) have just decided not to write a "challenge" for you.*

ACTION		OPTION
Avoidance	Avoidance	Neither option looks good.
Positive, but obstacle in way		Choose to get around, over, or under the obstacle.
Positive	Positive	Both choices look good.
Action dictated		No choice looks possible.

✎ Give an example of an avoidance/avoidance choice in your life.

_____

_____

_____

✎ Share an obstacle option and how you worked it out.

_____

_____

_____

✎ Write a positive/positive choice you had. What did you choose?

_____

_____

_____

Putting It Together. *What do I do if it looks as if I can do nothing? (No choices are possible.) When does this happen in my life? How did I feel about writing my own "challenges?"*

Spin Off. *Share some decision-making experiences that you have had and how you handled them. Use one of the methods from "Discussions and Debates" (pp. 77-78) to make a presentation to the total group.*

LIVE LIFE OR BE RUN BY IT?

> ***Challenge.*** *Can you imagine a horse walking down the street, pushing a cart in front of it? Can you also picture your life being controlled by everyone or everything around you? This is as ridiculous as a cart-drawn horse.*

Explore.

✎ List three areas where you have only a little voice in decision-making (if at all).

1. _____

2. _____

3. _____

✎ Decide which two of these areas most concerns you. Suggest some ways you would like to take more responsibility in these areas and how you would change it.

Area 1

_____

_____

_____

_____

Area 2

_____

_____

_____

_____

> ***Putting It Together.*** *How does it feel when I gain control of my own life? When does it happen? How? Why? How often? How can I do it more? Should I? Can I do it with love? Diplomatically? Planned, not reactive?*
>
> ***Spin Off.*** *Share one or two areas of decision-making over which you feel you have little control, and what you plan to do about it. Can you do it gently but firmly? Is confrontation "bad?"*

REMEMBERING

> ***Challenge.*** *Storing information in your brain is easy. The hard part is pulling information out of storage. It takes practice to get in the right mood to retrieve specific data or pictures.*

Explore.

✎ Read the following paragraph once and cover it up. Then answer the questions that follow without looking at the paragraph.

"The fires in the log and bark-covered longhouse threw flickering shadows on the carved masks of the false faces. These men of the solemn wooden countenances had danced around and through the fires for a day and two nights. The observers on the benches surrounding this tribal ritual had the glazed and entranced looks of those who look too long into the fire."

—from the novel "Holy Savages," by Dennis Hooker

1. The dancers are Native Americans. Yes _____No_____Don't Know_____

2. From what material are the masks made? _____

   _____

3. Give the writer's first name _____

4. Write your own "factual paragraph" ("make up" the facts). _____

_____

_____

_____

_____

_____

_____

_____

_____

_____

_____

_____

_____

_____

✎ Your paragraph will be read on a TV game show. Write ten questions to ask the contestants. (Be accurate.)

1._____

_____

2._____

_____

3._____

_____

4._____

_____

5._____

_____

6._____

_____

7._____

_____

8._____

_____

9._____

_____

10._____

_____

Spin Off. *You are a game show host. The Think Tank members are the panelists. Read your paragraph and ask your questions. See who answers the most correctly and quickly. Pick one member and one "game." Do this with the total group.*

YOUR CLASSMATES

Challenge. *Can you tell what a person is like by looking at them?*

Explore.

✎ Look at four people across the room from you. Decide what each is thinking and feeling. Humor is not desirable in this personal experience. Please be gentle and caring because four people are looking at you.

NAME	WHAT DOES THE PERSON SEEM TO THINK ABOUT?	WHAT DOES THE PERSON USUALLY FEEL?	WHY DID YOU KNOW THESE THINGS?
1.			
2.			
3.			
4.			

✎ Look at each of your classmates again. What would you like to know more about each of them?

1._____

2._____

3._____

4._____

Putting It Together. *Why would I want to know more about others? Why is it not easy to know the "innermost working" of others? Do I want others to know me? Why? What? When? How?*

Spin Off. *Gather into groups to share your thoughts and feelings with as many of the five persons as you can. What are the joys and hazards of getting close to others? Talk about it in the total group.*

USING GRAPHIC WORDS

> **Challenge.** *Most good words flash their visual image on the screen of your understanding. It is said, "One picture is worth a thousand words." It is also true that "One word can trigger a thousand pictures."*

Explore.

I [picture] so much of my [clock] [eye] 4 a [face]. What way to [traffic light]. What way to [lightbulb]. I want to hear choices about [faces]. I discover feelings [figure] and [face] and [figure].

✎ What do the pictures and words say?

_____

_____

_____

_____

_____

_____

©1991, JIST Works, Inc. • Indianapolis, Indiana

✎ Make a hieroglyphics message of your own. Put the finished product in the space below. Have the small group members read it and suggest possible changes to improve the message.

✎ Make a hieroglypics message from the paragraph below. Use scrap paper for the preliminary work.

I am tired of analyzing myself because I begin to have isolated feelings. I am stopping that and starting to have fun and satisfaction. I want to love and grow as a healthy plant does. I will accept responsibility for making my own choices.

Spin Off. *Work with your small group to combine the best of your symbols into a final message. Compare these with the other groups and make one final product that is displayed on the board*

Work with your small group to make a list of words that can be drawn as pictures. (Use a separate page.) Share them. Play charades with them. Use them often as you write or talk.

FEELINGS LIST

> **Challenge.** *You have experienced many different feelings during the course of your life. You are not the only person who has felt these feelings. Everyone has had feelings at some time or other. Try thinking of the feelings you have experienced.*

Explore.

✎ Underline the feelings you have experienced. Write the initial of someone you know who shares same feeling. *Example: M could be myself; S a sister; T a teacher.*

__ Abandoned	__ Cheated	__ Dominated	__ Gratified
__ Adequate	__ Cheerful	__ Doubtful	__ Greedy
__ Affectionate	__ Childish		__ Guilty
__ Agony	__ Clever	__ Electrified	
__ Almighty	__ Combative	__ Empty	__ Happy
__ Ambivalent	__ Competitive	__ Enchanted	__ Hateful
__ Angry	__ Condemned	__ Energetic	__ Heavenly
__ Annoyed	__ Confused	__ Envious	__ Helpful
__ Anxious	__ Conspicuous	__ Evil	__ Helpless
__ Apathetic	__ Contented	__ Excited	__ High
__ Astounded	__ Contrite	__ Exhausted	__ Homesick
__ Awed	__ Cruel		__ Honored
	__ Crushed	__ Fascinated	__ Horrible
__ Bad		__ Fearful	__ Hurt
__ Beautiful	__ Deceitful	__ Flustered	__ Hysterical
__ Betrayed	__ Defeated	__ Foolish	
__ Bitter	__ Delighted		__ Ignored
__ Bold	__ Desirous	__ Frantic	__ Impressed
__ Bored	__ Despair	__ Free	__ Infuriated
__ Brave	__ Destructive	__ Frightened	__ Inspired
__ Burdened	__ Determined	__ Frustrated	__ Intimidated
	__ Different	__ Full	__ Isolated
__ Calm	__ Discontented	__ Furious	
__ Capable	__ Distracted		__ Jealous
__ Challenged	__ Disturbed	__ Glad	__ Joyous
__ Charmed	__ Divided	__ Good	__ Jumpy

— Kicky
— Kind
— Keen

— Lazy
— Left Out
— Lonely
— Longing
— Loving (love)
— Low
— Lustful

— Mad
— Mean
— Melancholy
— Miserable
— Mystical
— Naughty
— Nervous
— Nice
— Nutty
— Obnoxious
— Obsessed

— Odd
— Opposed
— Outraged
— Overwhelmed

— Pain
— Panicked
— Peaceful
— Persecuted
— Pity
— Pleasant
— Pleased
— Pressured
— Pretty
— Proud

— Quarrelsome

— Refreshed
— Rejected
— Relaxed
— Relieved
— Remorseful

— Restless
— Reverent
— Rewarded
— Righteous

— Sad
— Satisfied
— Scared
— Screwed
— Settled
— Sexy
— Shocked
— Silly
— Skeptical
— Sneaky
— Solemn
— Sorrowful
— Spiteful
— Startled
— Stingy
— Stupid
— Stunned
— Suffering

— Sure
— Sympathetic

— Tempted
— Tense
— Terrible
— Threatened
— Tired
— Trapped
— Troubled

— Ugly
— Uneasy
— Unsettled

— Vivacious

— Weepy
— Wicked
— Wonderful
— Worried

Spin Off. *Share some of your experiences with others in your small group. Pick a couple of stories from your small group to share with the total group.*

FEELINGS BINGO

> **Challenge.** *Use the feelings you chose in the previous exercise to play the following adaptation of "Bingo."*

Explore.

✎ From the feelings list on the previous page, select feelings you have had yourself and put one in each of the squares of game 1 below. A leader will then select words at random from the feelings list and say them out loud. If the feeling they call matches one you listed on your game square, put an "X" through that box. When you have three in a row (down, across or at an angle), say "Bingo." Then repeat the process for games 2, 3 and 4. Draw your own squares for more games.

GAME 1		
1	2	3
4	5	6
7	8	9

GAME 2		
1	2	3
4	5	6
7	8	9

GAME 3		
1	2	3
4	5	6
7	8	9

GAME 4		
1	2	3
4	5	6
7	8	9

THE SPONGE

> **Challenge.** *A sponge opens to soak up. A clam clamps up to shut out. A person who is being complimented by someone should be like a sponge—not a clam.*

Explore.

✎ Pretend you are talking directly to the people listed below. Say two positive things that you really feel about the person. Imagine that they enjoy what you say and soak up your positive thoughts like a sponge.

THE PERSON	THE POSITIVE STATEMENT
A parent	1.
	2.
Another close relative	1.
	2.
A female friend	1.
	2.
A male friend	1.
	2.
An instructor/teacher	1.
	2.
Someone you don't really like	1.
	2.

> **Putting It Together.** *How do I like feeling positive thoughts about people I know? Negative thoughts? Am I positive enough? Where is it ok to think negatively?*
>
> **Spin Off.** *Talk about some positive feelings with your small group. Now, go to some of these people to share your thoughts and feelings. Accept the positive sharing of others as you would want them to accept yours.*

WORKING WITH OTHERS— SEEDS OF SERVICE

> **Challenge.** *In Section I of this book, you listed ways to increase your service to the world. It may be that no great or earth-shattering ideas have occurred to you yet. You may not see a hidden gem in your ideas for years to come.*
>
> *Imagining how you can help others in your community and the world will be necessary many times in your life because your ideas grow and your life changes.*

Explore.

✎ Write down ways you can work with others to help those in your community and the world.

_____

_____

_____

_____

_____

_____

_____

_____

_____

_____

_____

> **Putting It together.** *I will read over my responses and enjoy the seeds I have planted in my own mind. What service can I do now? How?*
>
> **Spin Off.** *Share all your ideas with your small group. Remember, no judgments or snickering. How can you work with others to help even more people? Share ideas. Assemble an "Experts Question" format (p. 77) to explore the idea of "Service." You may invite outside experts to question.*

SIMULATION II—*Our Business*

> **Challenge.** *In Simulation II—Our Business, you will make good use of your communication skills. In it, you will use the game you developed in the first simulation to create a product to share with the world.*
>
> *You have shared your thoughts and feelings with others in your small groups and in the large group. You have talked in depth with others, made individual and group decisions, and heard the feelings of other members as they have heard yours. And you have planned and completed projects alone and with others.*
>
> *You have gone beyond your own uniqueness to realize your similarities with others. You have been successful as your communication skills increased with your friends and team members.*

Explore.

✎ In Section I of this book, your group produced a successful game. In this simulation, you decide to organize your team into a company to produce and sell your game to others.

By now, you know the other members of the team and their areas of interest and expertise. Keep these in mind as you select team members to fill various jobs in your business such as president, secretary, treasurer, bookkeeper, marketing specialists, etc. Make a WORKABLE organization. You will decide:

—How to finance the business.   —The market (who, where, how, etc.).
—What price to charge.   —Other important issues.

Time Passes (after your organization is flowing and the product is functioning)

✎ Your business has become so successful that you need outside assistance to expand. You are trying to recruit members from other teams. Have your group interview them. Phrase your interview questions so that you see the person's strong points.

✎ You must hire two qualified people to help your company. What positions are needed? List the skills and training you seek in a new employee for each position.

_____

_____

_____

_____

_____

_____

Even More Time Passes and ...

✎ The demand for your game is good, but not overwhelming. You decide to combine your game with that of another team, a merger. Decide before you meet what is necessary to do business with another company. Do you have weak areas that you need to strengthen? Could your games be similar? Plan the criteria for meeting and doing business with this company for the proposed merger.

✎ Meet with the other small groups, exchanging proposals for the mergers. Decide on the company with whom you will merge. How will you handle it if another company also wants to merge with the company you choose (arbitration, compromise, buy-outs, etc.)?

_____

_____

_____

_____

_____

_____

_____

> ***Putting It Together.*** *Do I believe in this product? Why? Why not? What is my role in this product and process? Am I doing it? Why? How do I do it better? Could we actually market our game? How? When? What must happen first?*
>
> ***Spin Off.*** *What would be the next steps you would take if you were to take this project from the Simulation stage to an actual corporation to market your game in the "real world?" Discuss the feasibility of actually doing it! Yes... Actually doing it! Do you believe in your product? Your organization? If not, why?*

SMALL GROUP INVENTORY II

Challenge. Evaluate your small group.

Explore.

✎ Now that you have completed the second simulation in this book, express your opinions about the small group you have been working with. Think carefully how your group worked together. Work individually.

CHARACTERISTIC	CIRCLE ONE		
	LOW	AVG	HIGH
Level of Sincerity			
Your desire to do your best	1	2	3
Your attempt to learn more	1	2	3
Comments:			
Research			
Use of many sources	1	2	3
Clear, straight-forward sharing of material	1	2	3
Comments:			
Awareness			
Your attempt to listen to ideas of others	1	2	3
Level at which the group communicates ideas	1	2	3
Comments:			
Cooperation			
Level at which you work together	1	2	3
Understanding of needs of others	1	2	3
Comments:			
Product			
Completion of work	1	2	3
Clarity of work	1	2	3
Appearance of work	1	2	3
Comments:			
Your Overall Satisfaction With the Group	1	2	3
Comments:			

SELF-INVENTORY II

Challenge. *Evaluate yourself. How are you doing so far?*

Explore.

✎ Ask yourself these questions honestly and with a fair degree of self-examination.

CHARACTERISTIC	CIRCLE ONE		
	LOW	AVG	HIGH
My Level of Sincerity			
Desire to do my best	1	2	3
Attempt to learn more	1	2	3
Wish to cooperate	1	2	3
My Research			
Use of many sources	1	2	3
Clear, straight-forward responses in book	1	2	3
Attempt to find more resources	1	2	3
My Awareness of Self			
Discovering new things	1	2	3
Desire to improve	1	2	3
Working on personal challenges	1	2	3
My Awareness of Others			
Cooperation in groups and Think Tanks	1	2	3
Level of ability to communicate ideas	1	2	3
Ability to assist others	1	2	3
My Written and Oral Product			
Quality of oral report	1	2	3
Excellence of written work	1	2	3
Amount of preparation for oral or written work	1	2	3
The Carry-over Outside School			
Homework	1	2	3
Degree of interest in my studies	1	2	3
Hobbies and interests that relate	1	2	3
Overall Sense of Personal Satisfaction			
My satisfaction in my personal growth	1	2	3
Ability to be a friend increasingly	1	2	3
More awareness of the world	1	2	3
Amount of available energy used	1	2	3
Degree I progressed compared to my potential	1	2	3

Moving On

Now, after two sections of this book, you know much more about yourself and the group you have been working with. Through this section of the book and *Our Business* Simulation, you have discovered how you work within your group and the unique gifts you bring to the group.

In Section III, "Success in the World," you will see how successful you can be as you take your talents and those of your group to the world around you.

You may be surprised to find out that the world will see you and your group as successful. As you experience the following section, you will find success you may have never known before—the success of making a difference in the world.

Don't forget, there are no "right" or "wrong" answers, only differences of opinion.

SECTION III
Your Success In
The World

Section I of this book helped you learn more about yourself. In Section II, you shared many experiences with other people in your groups. Now in Section III, you look outside yourself and your group into the world itself. This is a world that NEEDS YOU and what you can offer. At the same time, you can learn even more about yourself to stretch your imagination even further.

As you have learned so far, success is merely the path you are on when you decide that you, yourself, are important. You don't have to compare yourself with others to be successful. And even "winning" or "losing" is not important to being successful.

Section III should show you that you do not have to prove yourself to anyone else.

In this section, you work toward the final simulation called *The Communique*. This simulation will have you develop a newsletter to the world. This simulation brings together all you have experienced and discovered in the earlier two sections of this book.

The Communique provides you with the ultimate challenge to share yourself, your ideas, your creativity, concern, and caring with the whole world.

DESIGN YOUR OWN EVALUATION

> **Challenge.** *Everyone receives grades or some form of evaluation in school and on the job. Until now you've had no voice in how you are evaluated. Now you do!*

Explore.

✎ You will design your own report card. Move into your small groups to brainstorm ideas for the new report card.

What we want to evaluate:

_____
_____
_____
_____
_____
_____
_____

The best way to design the evaluation card:

_____
_____
_____
_____
_____
_____
_____

> **Spin Off.** *Make a first draft. Exchange your card with other small groups.*

✎ List what you like about the other ideas that you might include in your own evaluation. Share your constructive criticisms with the other groups about their cards.

_____

_____

_____

_____

_____

_____

_____

_____

✎ Make a finished report card for yourself.

List the report card's assets:

1._____   4._____

2._____   5._____

3._____   6._____

✎ Changes you would still make to improve it (Do you want to make the modifications before you share it?).

_____

_____

_____

> **Spin Off.** *Share your finished report cards with the other small groups. Are there more similarities or differences?*

SHARING YOUR INTERESTS

> **Challenge.** *Many activities take place everyday at school and in the community. You may not know about them because they may not be advertised or promoted. You may be interested in music, art, sports, or construction. Perhaps you want to help people pursue spiritual and personal growth or find answers to problems.*

Explore.

✎ List two of your major interests:

1. _____

2. _____

✎ Where in your community can you get more experience or training in your area of interest? Research this, and ask around.

_____

_____

_____

_____

_____

_____

_____

✎ How can you become even better at your interests?

_____

_____

_____

_____

_____

_____

_____

> ***Putting It Together.*** *One of my interests may be marketable—I can make money at it now or in the future. I will think of ways to make one of my interests pay for itself now.*
>
> ***Spin Off.*** *Meet with your Think Tank. Brainstorm ways to start your own clubs for your interests. (Remember, brainstorming is listing your ideas as fast as you can without judging, analyzing or commenting on them as you write.)*

✎ Write your ideas down first. Then go back and think about each one.

_____
_____
_____
_____
_____
_____
_____
_____
_____

✎ Now, rank order your list.

_____
_____
_____

✎ Devise a plan to initiate one of your ideas.

_____
_____
_____

UNWRITTEN WORDS

> **Challenge.** *Write a story. The best stories are written **between** the lines.*

Explore.

✎ Decide what feelings you want your readers to have after reading your story. List the types of feelings between the lines of your story. Write words that will cause those feelings to occur.

_____

_____

_____

_____

_____

_____

_____

_____

✎ Choose a certain feeling that a reader may have. (Check the list of feelings on pages 92-93 in Section II of this book.) Think of a scene that is sure to leave the readers with that feeling and write it in the space below.

_____

_____

_____

_____

_____

_____

_____

✎ Use a separate sheet to write a one-page scene. Work on it until you feel confident the reader will develop a certain feeling during or after reading your scene.

> ***Putting It Together.*** *Do I have a good story? What does it need, if anything? Does it give me the feeling I want the audience to have?*

✎ Share it with two readers. Ask the readers to tell some feelings they have.

Reader #1 _____

_____

_____

Reader #2 _____

_____

_____

✎ Did you get the reaction you wanted? Yes ____No ____Explain.

_____

_____

_____

_____

_____

✎ Ask for suggestions to make the scene even better. List eight suggestions below.

_____

_____

_____

_____

_____

_____

_____

_____

> ***Spin Off.*** *Share with your small group. Did you get the responses you wanted? What could you have done differently? Read or act out one or two (or more) scenes from your small group in front of the total group.*

THE COURTROOM

> **Challenge.** *Some decisions must be made within the law of the courtroom. Laws should be fair to all parties.*

Explore.

✎ Move into small groups, and decide the following roles:

Judge: You run things fairly and your decision is final.

Prosecuting Attorney: You must convince the jury that the accused is guilty.

Defense Attorney: You must convince the jury that the accused is innocent.

Defendant: You are accused of the crime.

Plaintiff: You accuse the defendant of committing the crime.

Jury: You must decide whether the defendant is guilty or innocent.

✎ Choose a crime that might be committed. (Be very specific. Make it something about careers and/or school.) Brainstorm for the most interesting crime.

_____

_____

_____

_____

✎ Then, have the plaintiff and prosecuting attorney brainstorm their case.

_____

_____

_____

_____

✎ The defendant and defense attorney brainstorm their defense.

_____

_____

_____

_____

✎ Next, move your class desks and chairs to change the room into a courtroom.

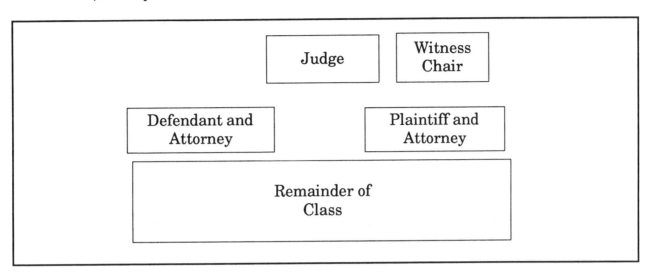

✎ Try the case!

> ***Spin Off.*** *Meet with your own small group to discuss all aspects of the case. List the suggestions to do it better. Compliment the positive aspects and the people involved. Now, try another case, and then do the Spin Off activity again.*

TWO SIDES TO AN ARGUMENT

> **Challenge.** *To maintain your integrity, sometimes you must take a definite moral and ethical stand. Other decisions are not so clear cut.*

Explore.

✎ Take a stand on the following statements:

	STRONGLY AGREE	???	STRONGLY DISAGREE
Gifts are not as appreciated as something we earn.			
Young men and young women think differently.			
School is a necessity of life.			
A person should achieve independence by age 20.			
Young children should be in bed by 7:00 p.m.			
Never say anything negative about something given as a gift.			
Two can live cheaper than one.			
The world is becoming a better place.			
An important issue of your choice:			
An important issue of your choice:			

> **Spin Off.** *Dramatize your moral or ethical stand. Use the following chair placement as a model. A moderator will read a statement and ask four people who "Strongly Agree" (Pros), four people who "Strongly Disagree" (Cons), and four people who "Not Sure" (???) to take a seat representing their stand on the issue.*

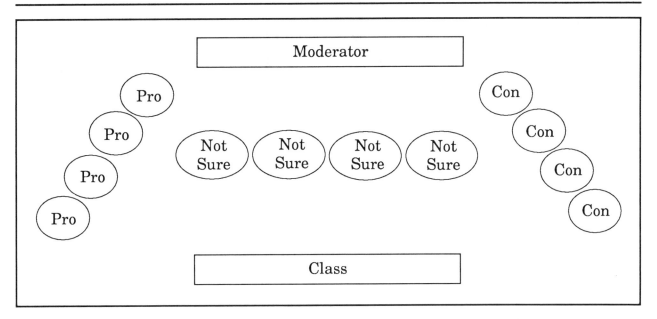

✎ Task 1. Pros and Cons are to convince the others of their way of thinking. At the end of five minutes, the "Not Sures" must take a stand as a "Pro" or "Con." "Pros" or "Cons" may switch if they decide differently.

✎ Task 2. The moderator reads a statement and asks people to sit in the chairs that represent their opposite view ("Pros" sit in "Con" chairs). They must convince others of their point of view — even though they don't really believe it.

> ***Spin Off.*** *Assemble in your small groups. Try to come to a concensus on each of the above issues. Can you? What alternatives do you have? Total group is to illustrate on the board or overhead, by vote, the decisions on each issue.*

LEARNING MODALITIES

> **Challenge.** *You are usually taught in school through your sight or your hearing. Persons with poor vision or hearing can easily become poor students. But, each of us is able to learn in many other ways.*
>
> *Good teachers are able to teach the same idea many different ways.*

Explore.

✎ The unit will include:
Simple audio-visual teaching aid.
5-10 minute lectures.
A short post-test.

✎ The total group is to subdivide in "Specialists" in that particular expertise of each modality. Examples:
Eyes: the eyeball, optic nerve, occipital lobe, etc.
Ears: outer ear, inner ear, cochlea, etc.
Kinesthetic: touch, smell, taste, balance, etc.
Extended Sensory Perception: fine tuning perceptions, biofeedback, hypnosis, etc.

✎ How do you begin your research?

_____

_____

_____

_____

✎ List some places you can find this information:

_____

_____

_____

✎ Name two outside "Specialists" who can help you gather information:
1._____
2._____

✎ Brainstorm with your Think Tank to come up with new ways to teach an idea or a concept.

_____

_____

_____

_____

_____

_____

> ***Putting It Together.*** *What are my strongest learning modalities? (Visual? Auditory? Kinesthetic? Extended Sensory Perception?) Weakest? How have I been taught? How can I improve my learning ability? How can I find out more about this area? How do I learn best? When? Where? Why? What?*
>
> ***Spin Off.*** *Discuss the progress and assignment of responsibilities until all roles are clear and tasks are ready to be presented. Assist the one(s) with problems. Get "second opinions." Make presentations to the class.*

THE BODY TALKS

> **Challenge.** *You usually show what you think by the words you say. But, you also send messages by the way you stand, move your arms, and use your face for expression. This is part of nonverbal communication. Experts say that up to 90 percent of your communication is nonverbal!*

Explore.

✎ Use the feelings you selected from your earlier Bingo game on page 94 to choose a feeling to act out with the group. Select a person to act out the first feeling. The person who first guesses the feeling correctly becomes the next actor. Do this until everyone has acted at least three or four times. Use the space below to describe what the actor did. Describe how different feelings were acted and your first guess. Then, write the feeling the person was acting out.

DESCRIPTION OF MOVEMENTS	FEELINGS I GUESSED	ACTUAL FEELINGS PORTRAYED

> ***Spin Off.*** *After 5 feelings are acted out, discuss how difficult it is to express a feeling to others. How could these problems interfere in communication with your family? Your friends? Your co-workers? Others? Think of solutions.*

✎ Act out 5 more feelings.

DESCRIPTION OF MOVEMENTS	FEELINGS I GUESSED	ACTUAL FEELINGS PORTRAYED

> ***Putting It Together.*** *How many times did I guess right or even close? What types of feelings were hardest to understand? Why? What feelings were the easiest to act out? Why?*
>
> ***Spin Off.*** *Share with your small group your thoughts from the "Putting It Together" section. Discuss the importance of knowing your own feelings and managing their expression.*

PRESENT YOUR VIEWPOINT

> **Challenge.** *You have taken a stand on certain key issues. You must now defend your position or viewpoint.*

Explore.

✎ In the earlier "Opinions" and "Do You Agree" exercises, you stated what you believe (list one or two emotional issues):

_____

✎ Find three to four other persons who feel as you do. Assemble the people who think alike into a Think Tank. Prepare to present your viewpoint to the class.

Describe a plan for the presentation:

_____

_____

_____

_____

✎ List the materials, facts, figures, or illustrations that you need for your presentation:

_____

_____

✎ List who is to do what:

_____

_____

> **Putting It Together.** *How did my feelings about the issues change as I worked together with others? Do others feel more strongly about important opinions than I do? Which issues?*
>
> **Spin Off.** *In your small group, discuss the advantages and disadvantages of taking strong stands. Why are concepts like "waiting," "moderation," "acceptance," "take it easy," and "is it important" important? When is "jumping right in," "taking a bold stand," or "being bold" important? Share your conclusions with the total group.*

COMPARE WITH HIGH STANDARD

> **Challenge.** *Find the writings of someone who has published an article that agrees with your opinion expressed in earlier experiences. (Use magazines, books, research journals, etc.) Write a short article (one page) about your opinion.*

Explore.

✎ List specific ways your opinion agrees with the published work:

_____

_____

_____

✎ List specific ways your opinion disagrees with the published work:

_____

_____

_____

✎ How would you judge whether an article is good or bad? Create five of your own standards that you would look for in a good article (i.e., clarity, consistency, etc.):

_____

_____

_____

✎ What rating do you give the published work (check one)?

❑ Excellent   ❑ Good   ❑ Fair   ❑ Poor

✎ What rating do you give your work (check one)?

❑ Excellent   ❑ Good   ❑ Fair   ❑ Poor

Putting It Together. *If I didn't do as well as I thought I could, what could I do to improve? I will brainstorm ideas, rank order and make a plan.*

Spin Off. *Work with your small group to make a checklist of things to look for in an article that makes it good. Share with other small groups to come up with a master list of "Qualities of a Good Article."*

Evaluate your own writing. Have two others read, and use the Master List to evaluate it.

©1991, JIST Works, Inc. • Indianapolis, Indiana

MY PLACE

> ***Challenge.*** *Your eyes are half closed ... you are very comfortable as you sit in your chair ... feel your body relaxing. Imagine yourself being in your own place—your own piece of the world ... it can be a place you have been to ... or it can be a place where you would like to be ... relax and allow your thoughts ... to ... wander ... freely ...*

Explore.

✎ Think about what you have just read; and as you relax, think about how you feel.

Now that you are relaxed, where are you? Describe it. _____

_____

Do you hear anything?_____

_____

Describe the feeling of the air around you._____

_____

What are you doing in this place?_____

_____

What feelings do you have? _____

_____

Is there anyone around you? _____

_____

What are they saying? Doing? _____

_____

Allow those people to see you and like you. What happens?_____

_____

> ***Putting It Together.*** *How do I like this feeling of relaxation?*
> ***Spin Off.*** *Share with the group what you have imagined.*

CURIOSITY

> **Challenge.** *You know yourself by comparing yourself with others. You usually do not find much difference between other people and you.*

Explore.

✎ To perform the following, you need:

1 shoe box with a lid	1 large card to stand up
2 pictures small enough to fit inside the shoe box	1 marker to write large letters

✎ Divide into teams. Each team is to paste a picture inside the end of a shoe box. Close the box, and stand a card near the box, labeled in large letters:

> Pretend this is really something!   Don't tell anyone!

✎ Label the box "Peeker Box" and place it where it can be seen by people who are not in your class. Place an identical picture on a wall near the box. Observe and record the number of "peekers" and their unique reactions. Interview some of the "peekers."

Which picture attracted the most viewers?_____

Why did it get more attention? _____

_____

Why is it more inviting to peek? _____

_____

Describe "curiosity." _____

_____

Who was the most curious? Least? _____

_____

> **Spin Off.** *Research how curiosity relates to learning. Work with your Think Tank to develop a report of your findings. Extract as much information as possible by using graphs, charts, and suggestions for improving the shoe box experiment (or devising similar tests to observe).*

 ©1991, JIST Works, Inc. • Indianapolis, Indiana

CLIFFHANGERS

Explore.

✎ Brainstorm a simple but exciting idea to expand into an outline for a play. Decide on the characters and plot. Write a two- or three-page cliffhanger where the thrilling conclusion ends prematurely—the reader is left hanging.

✎ Check one or two of these settings for your play.

✎ Brainstorm possible characters and plots. Then choose one from your list:

__ a stormy night	__ a dark forest	__ a forest fire
__ a graveyard	__ a blizzard	__ a volcanic eruption
__ a haunted museum	__ a flash flood	

CHARACTERS	PLOTS

Spin Off. *Share your cliffhanger with your small group. Assemble the cliffhangers into a book to loan through the library.*

YOU DECIDE

> **Challenge.** *You are suddenly given the ability to make people's lives turn out as you wish.*

Explore.

✎ Ellen has lived at home for 18 years and is just finishing high school. She has gotten along well with her parents, but she is beginning to feel an urge to go out on her own. She cannot pinpoint her anxiety, but she senses the urge to be independent. Finally, one day she approaches her parents and says:

_____

_____

_____

_____

_____

_____

_____

_____

_____

✎ Jim decided he needed to be making money by the time he was 18. His family had financial pressures that could only be relieved by Jim's helping out. He decided to look at all the options available to him at local schools. He had to have marketable skills by 18, or he would have to work at common labor jobs for less money. He decided to (you finish the story):

_____

_____

_____

_____

_____

_____

_____

_____

✎ Alice has wanted to work with blind children. She has felt this desire since she was 13 years old. She is now finishing high school and must decide on future training. Alice feels she cannot wait until she completes college to start working, but she knows a good education will open more doors for her. After much thinking and talking with advisors she decides to (you tell what to do):

_____

_____

_____

_____

_____

_____

_____

_____

✎ Dave is very intelligent, and he loves math and working with numbers. He is also very good with his hands—especially repairing machines. He cannot afford college and doesn't like sitting in a classroom for four hours or more. After much thought and talking with others, he chooses to (you tell what he does):

_____

_____

_____

_____

_____

_____

_____

_____

> ***Putting It Together.*** *How did I like having the power to give people's lives the ending I wanted?*
>
> ***Spin Off.*** *Discuss with your small group your story endings and whether you felt a sense of power as you made decisions about someone else's life. Share selected stories with the total group.*

WHAT DID PEOPLE DO WHEN THEY DIDN'T READ?

> ***Challenge.*** *"We live in a sensory environment totally different from that of pre-literate man—simply because we have learned to read. In shifting from speech to writing, man gave up an ear for an eye, and transferred his interest from spiritual to spatial, from reverential to referential."*
>
> ***—Edmund Carpenter***

Explore.

✎ Put this paragraph into your own words.

_____

_____

_____

✎ What are some disadvantages of experiencing life in a reading-oriented culture?

_____

_____

_____

✎ What would your personal thoughts be like if the world hadn't discovered reading?

_____

_____

_____

> ***Putting It Together.*** *I will imagine the advantages of living in a world where my life depended on finely tuned perceptions rather than book-learned knowledge. I'll jot down my thoughts.*
>
> ***Spin Off.*** *Share your ideas with others. Decide if reading has enriched or hindered life in general. Each Think Tank can create a short skit about a group of pre-literate people relying on their perceptions for survival.*

ROOTS

> **Challenge.** *Language is really the sum total of the languages of all your ancestors, and most words evolved from hundreds or thousands of years ago. At one point in history, all peoples probably lived together on one huge continent. As each went in a different direction, so did the variations of language.*

Explore.

✎ See whether your library has dictionaries of the following languages. Look up the words "man" and "woman" in the dictionaries you find. Then, look up the words "mother" and "father." Which words are similar in some languages and which words are different? If you or someone you know speak a different language, include these too.

French _____

German _____

Japanese (or another eastern language) _____

Spanish _____

Swahili (or some other African Language) _____

> **Putting It Together.** *I know myself by comparing myself with others. I usually find not much difference between other people and me. What are the similarities? Differences? How can that be good?*

✎ Work with your team to develop a list of words that describe a successful person. Look up those words in all the languages that you can find.

ENGLISH WORD	FOREIGN TRANSLATION

ENGLISH WORD	FOREIGN TRANSLATION

Spin Off. *Do you know someone who knows a language that does not appear on this list? Find words in that language that are the same (or similar) to words you have looked up in this exercise. Share with your class what you discover.*

FINE BLENDS

> ***Challenge.*** *Some languages began as a secret communication. For example, many Jamaicans can speak English with an Oxford accent. But when they were British slaves, native Jamaicans developed an expressive "underground" language that the English could not understand.*
>
> *Very few people are "native Americans." Even native Americans (or American Indians) must trace their roots to other continents. Do you know where your family came from?*

Explore.

✎ Find a language your ancestors may have spoken. Read about the language, and research its roots.

The language: _____

Its roots: _____

✎ To find out where your family came from, talk to your parents or grandparents or great aunts and uncles.

Can your family remember when someone in your family spoke another

language? _____

When did that person begin speaking English?_____

When? _____

How? _____

Why? _____

✎ Trace the roots of English. Diagram how far it goes back to a common tongue. What other languages developed from the same root? Use your dictionary to find words from as many different languages as you can.

_____

_____

_____

> ***Spin Off.*** *Get together with others in your class who have ancestors from the same part of the world. Prepare a short talk about your heritage for the class.*

SIMPLIFY THE COMPLEX

Challenge. *Cultivators of the Oriental Persimmon propagate the plant by grafting it onto rootstock. The seedling develops a long tap root; but the roots "sucker" prolifically. Seeds require stratification in moist peat.*

Explore.

✎ Rewrite the "Challenge" paragraph to make sense to a third-grade student, yet keep the meaning of the paragraph.

_____

_____

_____

✎ Work with one or two partners to rewrite an article from "GEO," "Discovery," "Scientific American" or a magazine of equal depth. Write it for a third grade class, simplifying the graphics. Make sure you use all the information, yet make it interesting to the class. Create, give, and grade short pre- and post-tests to see whether the class understood the presentation.

✎ Use sketches to *simplify* the ideas (practice on scratch paper, then transfer neatly to this lesson).

A HOUSEHOLD APPLIANCE	A LUNAR-TYPE LANDING SYSTEM

BICYCLE	MOUSETRAP

COMPLICATE THE SIMPLE

> **Challenge.** *The best learning takes place when your mind is relaxed, open, and interested.*

Explore.

✎ Rewrite the challenge paragraph to "stretch the brain" of a college senior.

_____

_____

_____

_____

✎ Work with one or two partners to rewrite an article or story from a first to third-grade level book. Write it at the level of a senior high school class. Keep the information intact, yet make it interesting to the class. Create, give, and grade short pre- and post-tests to see whether the class grasped the content of the presentation.

✎ Use sketches to *complicate* the following items (use scratch paper then transfer it neatly here).

A HOUSEHOLD APPLIANCE	A LUNAR-TYPE LANDING SYSTEM
BICYCLE	**MOUSETRAP**

ILLUSIONS

> ***Challenge.*** *You have been hired by an illusionist to write a short description of his optical illusions.*

Explore.

✎ Write one or two short sentences to describe each illusion for a book of optical illusions. Practice what you say verbally and on separate paper. Say it clearly, but briefly. You may label or number lines, angles, or circles to assist your description.

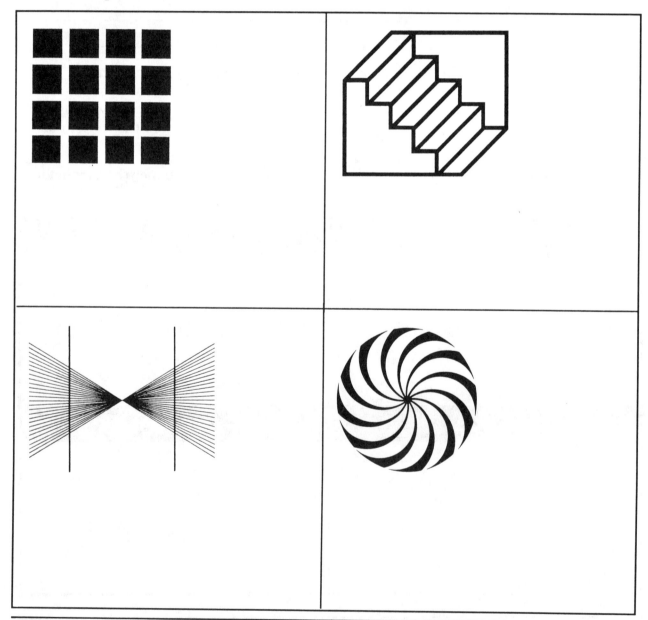

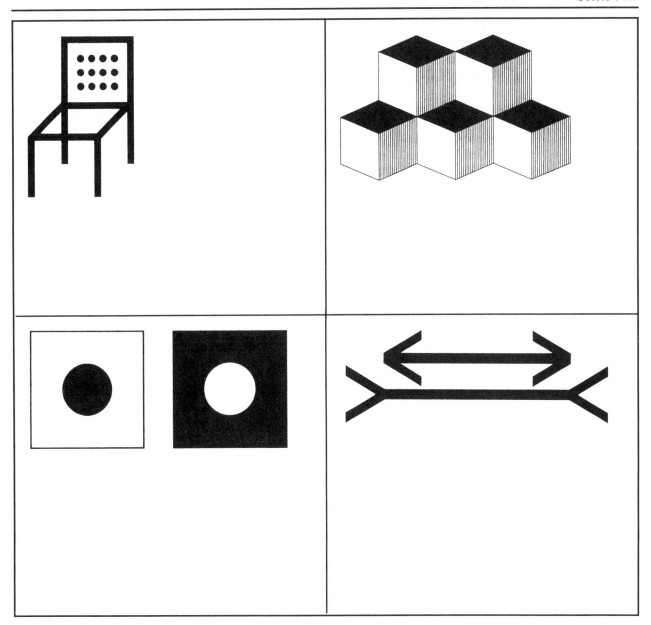

Putting It Together. *What am I doing here? This author (Hooker) must be totally _____. When, in my life, will I ever have to describe illusions? What value could it be? How did I do? Did I like it? Hate it?*

Spin Off. *Share your descriptions with your small group. Get and give suggestions. Pick a few to share with the total group.*

TECHNICAL WRITING

> ***Challenge.** Explain and describe the following illustrations.*

Explore.

✎ Describe how this Scale-o-brator™ works. Invent terms and parts.

_____

_____

_____

_____

_____

✎ Explain how to fly this glider.

_____

_____

_____

_____

_____

✎ How do you play this game? Give it a name.

_____

_____

_____

_____

_____

✎ Using separate paper, tell how to build this triangle.

_____

_____

_____

_____

_____

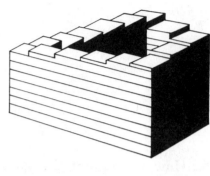

✎ Describe how to go down the stairs.

_____

_____

_____

_____

_____

✎ Explain the advantage of this "pair" of scissors.

_____

_____

_____

_____

_____

> ***Putting It Together.*** *What is most important about giving directions to someone else? I will look back at what I have written for this exercise. Could I have been more precise in my directions? Why should I?*

 ©1991, JIST Works, Inc. • Indianapolis, Indiana

DESCRIBING SIMILARITIES AND DIFFERENCES

> ***Challenge.*** *Some very different items have more in common than may be obvious at first. For example, how are an orange and a banana similar? They are both fruit is one correct answer. Another correct answer is that they can be eaten or peeled.*

Explore.

✎ Instead of looking for the differences between two different objects, find a similarity and a difference between each of the following groups of items:

GROUP	SIMILARITIES	DIFFERENCES
Toasters (example)	have heating elements	some toast 2 slices some toast 4 or more
Families		
Motivated students		
Aggressive people		
Creative or talented persons		
Methods of transportation		
Wars		
Eco-systems		
Political systems		
Loving people		
Food producers		

> ***Spin Off.*** *Share your answers with other students. Decide if each answer is the best possible.*

THIS IS YOUR PAGE

Challenge. *You have 15 minutes to yourself on this page.*

Explore.

Putting It Together. *What are my feelings, knowing that I am totally in charge of my own 15 minutes?*

Spin Off. *Share your "My Page" with the small group. Discuss the feeling of responsibility, having 15 minutes of your own.*

THOUGHTS AND FEELINGS

Challenge. *You can tune into your perceptions and feelings right now—at this very moment.*

Explore.

✎ NOW—What you see and hear (what your eyes and ears are experiencing) at this moment:

_____

_____

_____

_____

_____

_____

_____

_____

_____

_____

_____

_____

✎ NOW—What you think (the messages in your head at this moment):

_____

_____

_____

_____

_____

_____

_____

_____

_____

_____

_____

✎ NOW—What you feel (what is going on in your whole body at this moment):

THE FEELING	THE BODY LOCATION

Putting It Together. I will think of times when I get my thoughts mixed up with my feelings. What will I do about it?

Spin Off. Share your NOWs with other members of your small group. How are their NOWs different? Similar? Now, bring your NOW into the immediate "Now" (sharing what you discover with others in your group).

WHAT YOU WERE

> **Challenge.** *You are the result of all the people and factors that influence your life. You are the child of your parents who were the children of their parents. Besides all that, you have learned many behaviors that have become part of you that have little do to with your parents.*
>
> *So, you are the sum total of your heredity and your learned behavior—and you are MORE THAN THAT! You are a person who is different from anyone ever born. You are everything that has shaped you. But, you add your own uniqueness.*

Explore.

✎ List three things you do just like your parents. Do you walk the same as your father or sneeze as loudly as your grandfather? Do you laugh like your mother?

1. _____
2. _____
3. _____

✎ List three ways that you may have influenced your parents or changed their lives. What did they want to be when they were your age? Ask them.

1. _____
2. _____
3. _____

> **Putting It Together.** *How do I feel knowing that I am more than the sum total of my hereditary and learned behavior?*
>
> **Spin Off.** *Share with your small group. Who is responsible for your being who you are? Discuss how to respond to that person. Discuss "influences" in total group.*

WHAT YOU ARE

> ***Challenge.*** *You are different today. You are not the same as you were an hour ago. You are changing. You are different. Even your body cells are dying and being replaced at the rate of thousands per minute. Who you are can accurately be stated only at this very moment in time. You are a changing, dynamic individual—different from all others. And, you are different from who you were yesterday.*

Explore.

✎ List three ways you are different today from a year ago:

    1._____

    2._____

    3._____

✎ List three ways that you are the same as a year ago:

    1._____

    2._____

    3._____

> ***Putting It Together.*** *Are changes in my life occurring fast enough? Where? How? Why? Are changes too fast? When does it seem that way?*
>
> ***Spin Off.*** *Discuss these changes and differences with your group. Make a role playing skit about changes. Assemble a panel of experts to discuss "changes."*

WHAT YOU WILL BE

> ***Challenge.*** *Tomorrow you will be different from now. The change may be small and hardly noticeable—but you will change.*
>
> *In some ways, you change naturally, without conscious decision. Some situations force you to use rational thinking and imagination to change. You are always becoming YOU.*

Explore.

✎ List three ways you change naturally:

1. _____
2. _____
3. _____

✎ List three places in your life where you must change:

1. _____
2. _____
3. _____

> ***Putting It Together.*** *How much do I really want to change? In what areas? How? Who? What method?*
>
> ***Spin Off.*** *Discuss with your small group the changes in your life (occurring naturally and by choice).*

YOU WERE, ARE, AND WILL BE

> **Challenge.** *Consider what you have discovered about yourself.*

Explore.

✎ Write your thoughts about yourself as you were, are now, and how you imagine you will be.

I was: _____

_____

_____

_____

_____

_____

_____

I am: _____

_____

_____

_____

_____

_____

_____

I will be: _____

_____

_____

_____

_____

_____

_____

> **Spin Off.** *Share your thoughts with the group.*

SEEDS OF SERVICE III

Challenge. *Again you have the opportunity to focus on what you have to give, rather than on what you get.*

Explore.

✎ Brainstorm as many ways you can think of to serve others by giving of yourself. By writing these down, you have entered the Seeds of Service into your consciousness.

_____

_____

_____

_____

_____

_____

_____

_____

_____

_____

_____

_____

_____

_____

_____

_____

_____

Putting It Together. *I will look over these Seeds of Service every now and then. I will watch how these Seed ideas begin to influence my activities, hobbies, pastimes, career choices, service to the world, friendships, spiritual values, etc.*

Spin Off. *Share whether seeds planted in Seeds of Service I and II have already begun to "sprout" in your life. Discuss service. Listen to "testimonials" of change from total group members.*

TIME CAPSULE REVISITED

> **Challenge.** In Section I of this book, you were asked to write down important things about yourself. This would then be placed in a time capsule to be opened in 100 years. NASA had a problem with its capsule program, causing a long delay.

Explore.

✎ You are asked to completely rewrite your program for the time capsule. Use the thoughts and feelings you have discovered about yourself this year.

> **Spin Off.** Share your capsule narrative with the small group. What is different? How have you changed?

SIMULATION III— *The Communique*

The COMMUNIQUE

In Simulation I and II, you had to reach deep into your creativity and understanding of yourself to include others into your "circle of importance." You realized that feeling successful is an attitude that includes acceptance of who and what you ALREADY are. But, you also saw that your success requires that you deal with other people. You used these skills to create *The Game* and *The Business* in previous simulations.

In this third simulation, *The Communique,* you will communicate to the world. You will also think about what you can do to serve the world you live in. Language has been your tool to learn more about yourself. Now you will use language to share.

Creating *The Communique*

Your group has expanded to merge all the teams into one, large corporation. Your organization wants to help the world around you. You have decided to take on responsibilities to assist in public education, human rights, health and welfare, ecology, and other sensitive areas.

Meet as teams to discuss your commitment to the issues. Representatives from your group will coordinate with other teams' representatives to discuss and plan the corporation newsletter, *The Communique.* This multipage newsletter will present information, views and opinions, prospective programs, projections, etc. (These meetings will be conducted with all members of the Simulation teams.)

This newsletter represents the organization and will become the model for a quarterly publication. Your task is to take the simulation from the first, unpolished ideas and assignment of responsibilities, to an actual finished product.

The following list are newsletter positions that must be filled:

Managing Editor(s)	Printers/Typesetters	_____
Photographers(s)	Distributors	_____
Writers	Others	_____
Typists	_____	_____
Layout Artists	_____	_____
Advertising People	_____	_____

Do what is necessary to make the product. Devise periodic evaluations to see how the simulation is going.

If you are frustrated, bored, or "out-of-touch," meet with the assignment team to reflect, discuss, and make the project a satisfying process for you. YOU must assume the responsibility to make it work for you! Assist your co-workers in keeping on track.

Explore.

✎ List the problems you encountered and their solutions.

PROBLEM	SOLUTION

Putting It Together. What ways was developing this Communique satisfying to me? How do I truly feel? What would I do differently next time?

Spin Off. Congratulations! You have completed the newsletter. Share your thoughts about The Communique with everyone else in the class. Evaluate your newsletter according to criteria for good writing you have created in "Compare with High Standard," pp. 119-120. Before accepting your prize for completing three sections and simulations, evaluate your progress and the progress of the people in your groups.

SMALL GROUP INVENTORY III

> **Challenge.** *Share your evaluation of your small group.*

Explore.

✎ Now that you have completed the last simulation in this book, express your opinions about the small group you have been working with. Think carefully how your group worked together. Work individually.

CHARACTERISTIC	CIRCLE ONE		
	LOW	AVG	HIGH
Level of Sincerity			
Your desire to do your best	1	2	3
Your attempt to learn more	1	2	3
Comments:			
Research			
Use of many sources	1	2	3
Clear, straight-forward sharing of material	1	2	3
Comments:			
Awareness			
Your attempt to listen to ideas of others	1	2	3
Level at which the group communicates ideas	1	2	3
Comments:			
Cooperation			
Level at which you work together	1	2	3
Understanding of needs of others	1	2	3
Comments:			
Product			
Completion of work	1	2	3
Clarity of work	1	2	3
Appearance of work	1	2	3
Comments:			
Your Overall Satisfaction With the Group	1	2	3
Comments:			

SELF-INVENTORY III

> *Challenge.* How did you like your role in this simulation?

Explore.

✎ Ask yourself these questions honestly and with a fair degree of self-examination.

CHARACTERISTIC	LOW	AVG	HIGH
My Level of Sincerity			
Desire to do my best	1	2	3
Attempt to learn more	1	2	3
Wish to cooperate	1	2	3
My Research			
Use of many sources	1	2	3
Clear, straight-forward responses in book	1	2	3
Attempt to find more resources	1	2	3
My Awareness of Self			
Discovering new things	1	2	3
Desire to improve	1	2	3
Working on personal challenges	1	2	3
My Awareness of Others			
Cooperation in groups and Think Tanks	1	2	3
Level of ability to communicate ideas	1	2	3
Ability to assist others	1	2	3
My Written and Oral Product			
Quality of oral report	1	2	3
Excellence of written work	1	2	3
Amount of preparation for oral or written work	1	2	3
The Carry-over Outside School			
Homework	1	2	3
Degree of interest in my studies	1	2	3
Hobbies and interests that relate	1	2	3
Overall Sense of Personal Satisfaction			
My satisfaction in my personal growth	1	2	3
Ability to be a friend increasingly	1	2	3
More awareness of the world	1	2	3
Amount of available energy used	1	2	3
Degree progressed compared to my potential	1	2	3

YOU ARE SUCCESSFUL— SOME FINAL THOUGHTS

> ***Challenge.*** *You are different from what you were as you began this book. Your brain cells have made a complete change, your attitude is better, and you interact and communicate more effectively with other people in your group.*

Explore.

✎ List four major things you have learned about yourself:

1. _____

2. _____

3. _____

4. _____

✎ List what you have learned about your communication with others:

_____

_____

✎ Describe how you can better serve the world:

_____

_____

✎ What image do you have of yourself after you completed the exercises in this book? Has it changed?

_____

_____

> ***Putting It Together.*** *How do I feel about what I learned about myself? How can I use what have I learned about communication with others to interact more effectively with people? Am I better off after experiencing "I Am (Already) Successful?"*
>
> ***Spin Off.*** *Share your positive self-concept with others in the group—what was it like before? What happened? What is it like now? Thank everyone. You have done well!*

Congratulations!

In "The Wizard of Oz" the Tin Man thought he needed a heart—but all he needed was a ticking pocket watch and confidence. The Straw Man thought he needed a brain—but all he needed was a diploma and recognition. The Lion thought he needed courage—but all he needed was a medal and someone to believe in him.

They each learned that they were already successful. Each character just needed official recognition of qualities that were already there.

This, therefore, is your official recognition! Congratulations! You are already successful!

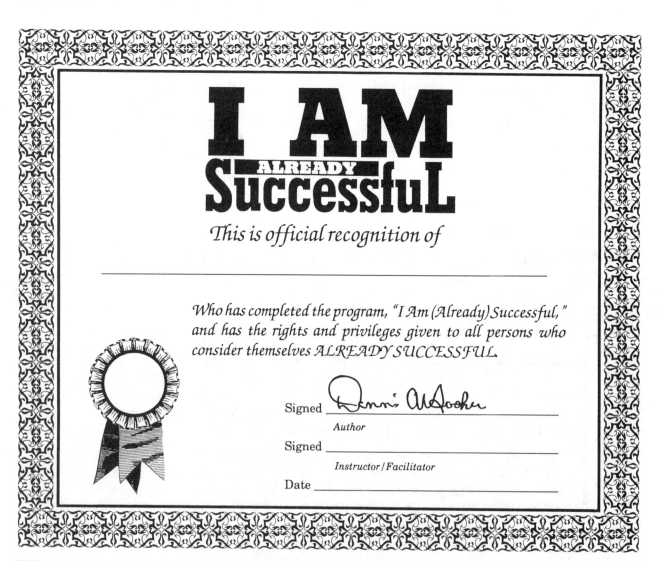

Notes:

Notes:

More Good Books from JIST Works, Inc.

JIST publishes a variety of books on careers and job search topics. Please consider ordering one or more from your dealer, local bookstore, or directly from JIST.

Orders from Individuals: Please use the form below (or provide the same information) to order additional copies of this or other books listed on this page. You are also welcome to send us your order (please enclose money order, check, or credit card information), or simply call our toll free number at **1-800-648-JIST** or **1-317-264-3720.** Our FAX number is **1-317-264-3709. Qualified schools and organizations** may request our catalog and obtain information on quantity discounts (we have over 400 career-related books, videos, and other items).
Our offices are open weekdays 8 a.m. to 5 p.m. local time and our address is:

JIST Works, Inc. • 720 North Park Avenue • Indianapolis, IN 46202-3431

QTY	BOOK TITLE	TOTAL ($)
_____	*Getting the Job You Really Want*, J. Michael Farr • ISBN: 0-942784-15-4 • **$9.95**	_____
_____	*The Very Quick Job Search: Get a Good Job in Less Time*, J. Michael Farr • ISBN: 0-942784-72-3 • **$9.95**	_____
_____	*America's 50 Fastest Growing Jobs: An Authoritative Information Source* • ISBN: 0-942784-61-8 • **$10.95**	_____
_____	*America's Top 300 Jobs: A Complete Career Handbook* (trade version of the *Occupational Outlook Handbook* • ISBN 0-942784-45-6 • **$17.95**	_____
_____	*America's Federal Jobs: A Complete Directory of Federal Career Opportunities* • ISBN 0-942784-81-2 • **$14.95**	_____
_____	*The Resume Solution: How to Write and Use a Resume That Gets Results*, David Swanson • ISBN 0-942784-44-8 • **$8.95**	_____
_____	*The Job Doctor: Good Advice on Getting a Good Job*, Phillip Norris, Ed.D. • ISBN 0-942784-43-X • **$5.95**	_____
_____	*The Right Job for You: An Interactive Career Planning Guide*, J. Michael Farr • ISBN 0-942784-73-1 • **$9.95**	_____
_____	*Exploring Careers: A Young Person's Guide to over 300 Jobs* • ISBN 0-942784-27-8 • **$19.95**	_____
_____	*Work in the New Economy: Careers and Job Seeking into the 21st Century*, Robert Wegmann • ISBN 0-942784-19-78 • **$14.95**	_____
_____	*The Occupational Outlook Handbook* • ISBN 0-942784-38-3 • **$16.95**	_____
_____	*The Career Connection: Guide to College Majors and Their Related Careers*, Dr. Fred Rowe • ISBN 0-942784-82-0 • **$15.95**	_____
_____	*The Career Connection II: Guide to Technical Majors and Their Related Careers*, Dr. Fred Rowe • ISBN 0-942784-83-9 • **$13.95**	_____
_____	*Career Emphasis: Making Good Decisions* • ISBN 0-942784-10-3 • **$6.95**	_____
_____	*Career Emphasis: Preparing for Work* • ISBN 0-942784-11-1 • **$6.95**	_____
_____	*Career Emphasis: Getting a Good Job and Getting Ahead* • ISBN 0-942784-13-8 • **$6.95**	_____
_____	*Career Emphasis: Understanding Yourself* • ISBN 0-942784-12-X • **$6.95**	_____
_____	*Career & Life Skills: Making Decisions* • ISBN 0-942784-57-X • **$6.95**	_____
_____	*Career & Life Skills: Knowing Yourself* • ISBN 0-942784-58-8 • **$6.95**	_____
_____	*Career & Life Skills: Your Career* • ISBN 0-942784-60-X • **$6.95**	_____
_____	*Career & Life Skills: Career Preparation* • ISBN 0-942784-59-6 • **$6.95**	_____
_____	*Living Skills Series: Effective Communication Skills* • ISBN 1-56370-038-7 942784-57-X • **$7.95**	_____
_____	*Living Skills Series Why Should I Hire You?* • ISBN 1-56730-039-5 • **$6.95**	_____
_____	*Living Skills Series: The Two Best Ways to Find A Job* • ISBN 1-56370-040-9 • **$6.95**	_____
_____	*I Am (Already) Successful*, Dennis Hooker • ISBN 0-942784-41-3 • **$6.95**	_____
_____	*I Can Manage Life*, Dennis Hooker • ISBN 0-942784-77-4 • **$8.95**	_____
_____	*Young Person's Guide to Getting and Keeping a Good Job*, J. Michael Farr & Marie Pavlicko • ISBN 0-942784-34-0 • **$6.95**	_____
_____	*Job Savvy*, LaVerne Ludden• ISBN 0-942784-79-0 • **$10.95**	_____

Subtotal _____

Sales Tax _____

Shipping: (*$3 for first book, $1 for each additional book.*) _____

(*Prices subject to change without notice*) (*U.S. Currency only*) **TOTAL ENCLOSED WITH ORDER** _____

☐ Check ☐ Money order   Credit Card: ☐ MasterCard ☐ VISA ☐ AMEX

Card # (if applies)_____ Exp. Date _____

Name (please print)_____

Name of Organization (if applies) _____

Address _____

City/State/Zip_____

Daytime Telephone (____) _____ — _____

Thank-you for your order!